How to Make A

MILLION DOLLARS

In Your
Home Service Business

Discover The Secrets To A Six

Figure Income From

A Front Line Entrepreneur

by Bob Burnham

Table of Contents

Introduction

The service business has afforded me the life many have only dreamed about. It is a business where once you understand the rules and universal customer service laws, there is absolutely no ceiling on income. My first home service business, a carpet cleaning venture, grossed over 25 million dollars and this by the time I was just thirty.

The marketing principles in this book work for any home service business and anyone, with little or no experience, can take the information in this book and duplicate the results. Most of it is common sense. Unfortunately, I guess, common sense is just not that common anymore!

I felt that writing this book was my duty to the fellow entrepreneur in the service business, to help break the cycle of pain and low-income results that at least 98% of companies in service businesses industry experience today. Most service companies are just barely surviving, financially and mentally.

These overworked service professionals are trapped by a cycle of customers who become harder and harder to satisfy with each passing year. Many service professionals, if they don't go broke after many years of struggling, are broken by the business and get out altogether.

These battle weary professionals are doing many things right and most are great people, but because they don't know some simple customer truths they are doomed to failure.

With just a few small changes they could turn money-losing, hour-gobbling, businesses into cash generating machines.

As I travel around the U.S., I have noticed some universal laws of service being violated to the detriment of the service business owners. They cannot see through their customers' eyes and it is costing them, big time.

It is the many little silver bullets of service conduct that can determine if they become financially independent. Each little change will add higher paying customers to their biggest asset, their customer lists.

Some business owners think that a little marketing is the only advertising effort that they need to acquire new customers. The fact is, marketing is a big part of everything that you do when your customer is hiring your service. If you run your company to "wow" your customers they will do a lot of your marketing and advertising for you for free.

You will always attract a better customer when your current customers are cheerleaders for your business. Blowing your own horn is only one thousandth as effective as when your customer is bragging about you. Word of Mouth (or Mouse!) can attract your best and most profitable customers. If you run your service business with the intention of exceeding your customers' expectations you will not be disappointed.

Don't become overwhelmed by all the strategies in this book because that will only stop you from moving forward. Take one strategy at a time and practice it until it becomes a new habit, bringing positive results to your company.

I wish you all the success that I have experienced in the service business over the years. Enjoy the journey!

Acknowledgements

This book is written with the help of many people, including some who know me well and some who have never heard of me before. It is through the many self-help, marketing, business, and non-fiction books I have read that have moulded the book you are about to read.

Dan Poynter, in his book 'The Self-Publishing Manual: How To Write Print and Sell Your Own Book," states a statistic that is hard to believe in this day and age. He claims that 58% of the U.S. adult population never reads a book after high school. So it is with this statistic in mind that I want to thank you for reading this book. You are already ahead of 42% of the adult population by just reading and making it possible for me to do what I do.

It is with great thanks and appreciation that I thank Jeff McCallum, my business partner, who has given me the opportunity through his wisdom, encouragement, and support to be able to bring you this book. It would have taken years longer without his support and I will always be indebted to him.

I also have to thank my family. To Marilyn, my wife, who should be awarded the badge of honour for pointing out my strong points and believing in me. To my daughters, Shay, Lex and Sky, who are the biggest reasons for me wanting to excel so that I may be an example of unconditional love, kindness, and encouragement.

I want to thank my coworkers at ABK Restoration Services and BurnMac Services, Lindsay, Tim, Brian, Sandy, Bruce, Ralph, Peter, Darren, and Joe. You guys are a daily inspiration to me.

Lastly, I want to thank my lawyer, Rick Watts, for always bringing me back to reason even before I was able to do it for myself, and to Jerry Miachika, my accountant, for his years of work and sound advice during the good and not so good times.

About the Author

Bob Burnham is the founder of ABK Restoration Services and BurnMac Services and lives In Coquitlam, British Columbia, Canada.

He is a former drummer of rock bands having toured Ontario, Canada before moving to Vancouver BC where he started a carpet cleaning company. The company eventually grew to 26 locations across Canada, generating $25 million in sales before Bob was 30 years old.

Bob sold his chain of carpet cleaning companies in the mid 1980's and later started both a chain of dog grooming stores and a smaller fire and flood restoration company.

It was the transition from owning a large company of 600 full and part time employees to running a much smaller company, that started him on the search for balance in his business life.

Bob has read hundreds of books on marketing, self-help, and spiritual topics to better help him live the true meaning of his dreams. He also listens to and owns a large library of CD's and cassettes on business related topics, which he frequently listens to while driving. He claims to have earned the equivalent of three PhD's just through his driving time over the last decade. Bob goes to several business related seminars every year and is always in touch with the latest business strategies.

It is through his constant and continued education that he has dedicated himself to the pursuit of helping others succeed in business in an easy and relaxed manner for the good of all people.

As Zig Zigler says:

"Help enough people get what they want and you will get what you want."

Chapter 1

The Millionaire Mindset

VICTIM OR VICTOR? IT IS ALL IN YOUR MIND

"Our attitudes control our lives. Attitudes are a secret power working 24 hours a day, for good or bad. It is of paramount importance that we know how to harness and control this great force."

—Tom Blandi

Mindset is something that is not taught in our traditional schools and yet it is the very reason some people have nothing but problems and some people do nothing but win and have great success in their lives.

Your **_Mindset_** is the software that was programmed into your subconscious mind as a child by your parents, teachers, coaches and surroundings, which is usually completely installed and running on autopilot by the age of eight. With these habitual thoughts, we create our daily living experience day in and day out.

We have as many as 60,000 to 80,000 thoughts per day. The good news is it shows how much we use our minds but the bad news is most of those 1,000's of thoughts are the same ones every day. If you are blissful and happy and have your ideal life I recommend you don't change any of your thoughts. If you are like the vast majority of our humans and you don't like what you see as your life, you need to change your thoughts, your <u>mindset.</u>

"If You Keep Thinking What You Think, You Will Keep Getting What You Get."
In other words the same mind that has created your problems in life will not be able to get you out of your current situation.

"If You Think Differently, You Will Do Differently."
You must be willing to change your mind and let in a new mind that will get you exactly what you truly want and deserve in your life. You must be willing to unlearn all the beliefs that are not helping and relearn new beliefs that will take you wherever it is you truly want to go in life.

Most of us and I am talking about 95% or more of the population, never stop to question the information we have been programmed with and go throughout our lives in an unconscious state of mind.

Now you might be asking at this point why I am talking about mindset when this is a book to help your business increase profits through marketing. Simply put, until you have an open mindset you will take this information, run it through the same old computer program, "your subconscious mind," and get the same old results you are programmed to getting.

You can't get different results with the same old mindset. You have to be open to new ways of thinking, being and doing. The only difference between Donald Trump and yourself is the way you think. If you thought like "the Donald" you would be like "the Donald." It is that simple.

Just recently in British Columbia, the province in which I live, we had an illegal teachers' strike. I heard the Union President say on TV that there was a long history in our province of the labour unions having to fight for what they got. When you think you have to fight for everything you get, you quite naturally get into a lot of fights. Maybe she likes fighting but I doubt it. She has probably been open to finding out that there are other ways in this world to acquire any, and every, thing you want.

As for the people on strike, the ones who are teaching our children, I think they do a tremendous job, generally speaking. But it is their fighting attitude that really keeps them from being everything they can be. And that is an attitude they may be passing on to our children.

Mindset is how you see the world. Do you see all the good, wealth, health and happiness around you or do you see problems, unhappiness and struggle? The most of the population only see the problems and don't realize they have a choice on how they see the world.

Because they are not aware of the fact they have freewill to choose their thoughts, they become victims and most often imprison themselves for a lifetime. They have no idea they themselves hold the key to the jail.

We can choose to be powerless victims of a government who is an oppressor that keeps us broke through over taxing, over regulating and political favours to the ones they like. Or we can choose to direct our own lives through our thoughts of self-management, which will create thoughts and actions to creating a reality of our liking.

When you give up being a victim and start choosing to be a victor your whole life will change and miracles will come to you on a daily basis.

As you think so shall you be.

WHAT YOU FOCUS ON EXPANDS

Said in other ways:
"What you dwell upon you become."
"You are the sum total of your thoughts."

"We become what we think about."
"We become what we repeatedly do."
> — *Aristotle*

"You are what you think about all day long."
> — *Dr. Robert Schuller*

"Change your thoughts and you change your world."
> — *Norman Vincent Peale*

"The greatest discovery of my generation is that a human being can alter his life by altering his attitudes of mind!"
> — *William James*

As you can see, by the many people who have practiced this most important breakthrough of the mind, it is not new to us. In fact, philosophers were saying this thousands of years ago, and yet in many cases it still remains a secret. It is a secret because even though it is information readily available to us all, there are still very few people that hear it.

There is a whole industry of self-help motivational material, coaches, teachers, and gurus that teach only this one principal because it is so powerful.

Earl Nightingale produced the famous recording "The Strangest Secret," which is the origin of the quote "We become what we think about." It is so obvious and yet 95% of us don't realize this, which indeed does make it a strange secret.

This one concept is so powerful, that once truly understood, it changes lives miraculously. It shows us how important our thoughts are and to always be aware of what we are creating in our lives by the thoughts we think.

Everything is brought into our world twice, first in thought and then in the physical form. The Wright brothers had to have an idea for an airplane and then it is from that thought they built the airplane into the physical form. At one time everything around you was first an idea in someone's mind.

The Wright brothers didn't just happen to be walking down the street one day and say to each other, "Look over there. I think we just discovered the airplane." Edison didn't just walk into a room, flick a switch and say, "I just discovered a light bulb."

New high tech inventions don't just drop out of the sky to be discovered by the nearest person. We create everything through our thoughts. Even though quantum physicists have known this for years, it seems to have escaped the general public who think that life happens to them instead of understanding they are create their own circumstances.

The naysayers are, by now, saying "There is no way I could create the situation I am living in today." Here's where the tricky part comes in. Most people focus their thoughts on what they don't want rather than what they do want.

Let me give you an example. Many of us say, "I hope I am not short of money at the end of the month to pay my bills." We say this month after month. Notice where the focus is when we do this? It's on being short of money at the end of the month.

Remember that what we focus on expands. Do you want your 'short of money' attitude to expand so you have even less at the end of the month? If instead, we told ourselves that we always have enough money and savings at the end of the month because of the many sources of income we attract and generate, we would have the outcome we truly want. This thought puts us in the attraction mode to learn and investigate ever-increasing sources to make an even higher income.

Once you open your mind to new possibilities and create a new mindset, you will to see the world as a wealthy and prosperous place that has limitless possibilities. The world, once limited by a closed mind, becomes a limitless world of miracles and opportunities. Soon you will wonder why you were so stuck in your own limited reality.

YOU WERE BORN RICH

In Bob Proctor's book "You Were Born Rich," Bob explains how we are all born rich but through incorrect programming when we are growing up, we lose the ability to be rich.

Bob makes the point that the only difference between someone who makes $50,000 per year and someone who makes $500,000 per year is the fact that the $50,000 per year person is not aware of the fact that he can make more money. He has thousands of testimonials from people who have gone from making little money to becoming rich. What stands in the way of becoming rich is buying into beliefs that we begin to see as truths, which stop us dead in our tracks.

We let beliefs such as, "I'm too old, I'm too young, poor, busy, sick or scared" stop us from living our dreams. You don't want to tell Jenny Wood-Allen of Scotland she is too old. She completed a London marathon at the age of 90 years old. You don't want to tell Loral Langemeier she is too young. Loral started a business as a single mom in college and was a millionaire by the age of 34. How about Mary Youngblood who went from welfare mom to Grammy award winner for best Native American album? Being too busy did not stop family man John Dressauer, father of two, from quitting a corporate job, starting his own business, and becoming a multi-millionaire within two years. Too sick? Tell that to Lance Armstrong who had cancer and went on to win the Tour De France seven times. And how about too scared? I guess you would have to talk to Stacy Allison who was the first American woman to climb Mount Everest.

These and a thousand different beliefs can be what are standing in your way to a life of wealth, health and happiness. The wealth, health and happiness is already here for us, but because of our beliefs, programmed into us by well meaning people when we were growing up, we resist them.

I am here to guarantee you that it is only your mind and your current beliefs that stand in the way to you creating the exact dream life you desire. Success and happiness start from the inside and then manifest on the outside. Once you have an open mind and are open to new possibilities and knowledge, it is just a matter of learning and choosing from the many different possibilities to create the exact life that you want.

When you are on the path to creating the life of your dreams and you experience resistance, it always stems back to a belief you have about what you are facing. If you identify that limiting belief and replace it with thoughts of possibility, you will always keep moving forward. Remember it is not the circumstance that stops you but rather how you view the circumstance. We always have a choice in how we view each circumstance.

There is a story about two women who worked in a large department store in customer service. Both had worked there for many years and over the years both were becoming depressed and discouraged with their jobs.

They were the women who had to respond to customer complaints and refunds for all the merchandise in the store. They heard customer after customer complain about broken products, bad service, and complaints about how customers had been treated. It reached a point where the two women were so bitter and burnt out that they gave their two weeks notice of resignation.

They had a talk with each other and decided that since they were leaving in two weeks time, they would just smile and be happy no matter what any of the customers said to them. Regardless of how mad, angry, or discourteous a customer was to them, they just smiled and kept their happy and blissful mindset.

Within a few days the women started to notice that the customers were acting different and were actually very polite and happy. By the end of the first week prior to their resignation they discovered that the customers were so happy and pleasant to deal with that the women decided to continue working at the department store because they once again began to love their work and like the customers again.

An change in their attitude caused an accidental change in their mindset, and they realized they themselves were creating the circumstances they were experiencing and not the customers at all.

You hold the thoughts that are reflected back to you like a mirror. You don't have to wait for people to be nicer. You are the creator of your mindset and so you must make the first move, by being nicer. Remember, anger begets anger and love begets love. Whatever you want, just give it away. Be the change you want to see and your whole world will open up to you.

FIGHTING FOR YOUR RIGHTS TO BE BROKE AND STUPID, AND THE WINNER IS THE "VILLAGE IDIOT"

"Argue for your limitations and, sure enough, they are yours"

Once you change your beliefs, you will begin to see and hear things in a different way. It is time for us all to stop fighting for our rights to be broke and stupid. Stop it and stop it now. We just don't need any more "village idiots."

We see things in our lives not as they are but as we are. Challenge every thought you have and see whether it is moving you forward or away from who you really want to be. Literally wake up and stop running on autopilot with thoughts that just don't serve you. Your thoughts are just habits you have formed and have taken on a life of their own.

It takes approximately twenty-one days to change a habit. First, you must identify a thought habit and then change it so that your automatic thought response is something that helps you move forward to who you were meant to be, rather than a habitual thought that keeps you broke and stupid.

Following is the four-step process you can use to change your habitual thoughts that will attract health, wealth, and happiness to you like a giant electro magnet.

Unconsciously incompetent
Consciously incompetent
Consciously competent
Unconsciously competent

1. An unconscious thought is a thought that was put into your mind as a child that you took as a truth or belief into your subconscious mind. It is a habitual thought that is not helping you move yourself forward. You

are *Unconsciously Incompetent* at this point in awareness.

2. You now take that thought and become aware or conscious of it, which will make you conscious of the thought but it is still not a thought that is helping you move forward in your life. You are *Consciously Incompetent* at this point in your awareness.

3. Your now conscious thought is changed to a better thought that moves you forward in life taking you where you want to be. You are now *Consciously Competent* at this point in awareness.

4. This is where the work comes in because you have to wrestle with the new thought until it becomes a new habitual thought. Once it is your automatic habitual thought you become *Unconsciously Competent* in you subconscious mind.

Your job in life is to program yourself with thoughts that will get you to a place in life you truly want to be. It can be one of the hardest things you will ever do but it is also the most rewarding to your health, wealth, and success.

Everyone is capable but it is a job only you can do for yourself. You only have to be open to the limitless possibilities that are available to us all. Success is an inside job. Only you can see what you are.

Chapter 2

The Emperor Has No Clothes

THE BLIND LEADING THE BLIND

Never be fooled by what the crowd is doing because many times in history the crowd has been wrong, just like in the story of "The Emperor Has No Clothes." In that story it took a child's eyes to see what was really happening and to say the truth.

We are at a good time in history to point out how often in our society we see the blind leading the blind. There is so much expertise for us all to draw on in our business that it always makes me laugh when I see people taking advice from others on business matters who have no experience in those areas.

Back in the late nineties, we have a really good example of this phenomenon. Dot Com companies were raising billions of dollars in share values because people were convinced from listening to the other uninformed village idiots about how it was a new economy and how all the old rules of business had changed.

People were investing their life savings in companies that did not have a business plan or even a business model to work from. People were mortgaging their houses, borrowing money, and getting money anywhere they could to invest into the latest Dot Com offering.

I started to notice that everybody and their sister was an expert at making money on the high tech stock market. The guy who cut my grass was giving me investment advice on how I could get rich in the stock market. By the way, anyone can become an expert and we cover this later in the book.

Stockbrokers were saying that even Warren Buffet, the second richest man in the world through stock investing, was losing touch because he was not in on this hot new trend in investing. Even my wife kept saying that we should invest in some of these highly speculative high tech stocks because we were losing out and many of our friends were making money, on paper that is. It was getting pretty tough to listen to and even I may have begun to doubt myself for a minute thinking that I might be missing out. NOT!

You see, something Warren Buffet, myself, and many other people knew were that these companies did not actually have a working business model. They did not have a working model that actually made money and produced profits. Looking back, some of these company plans were so ridiculous you wonder how anybody thought they were going to make money. Don't get me wrong, there are lots of companies on the Internet that make lots of money, but that is because they have good working and profitable business models and plans. These "Dot Bomb" companies were invested into based on pure hype from one greedy sucker telling the next greedy sucker until finally they ran out of greedy suckers and the Dot Com companies had to make money the real way with a real business. Thus, the Dot Bomb crash.

As I am writing this, I think we are now in a very similar situation with the real estate market in North America, where totally inexperienced investors are buying three and four properties because they have gotten tips from other inexperienced people, and on and on it goes. When we run out of suckers there is going to be a big price to pay. They will be in over their heads and will not be able to get rid of their properties for any price for a while. Luckily, the experienced people who take the time to learn the business will be fine. I realized the situation was happening after hearing that the guy who cuts my grass is now a real estate investor.

I must caution you that there are a lot of coaches and mentors who are willing to charge you a lot of money for advice, and in many cases, will leave you worse off. I also caution you from even being mentored by someone who is already working in your sector. They may look successful but there is at least a 95% chance that they are barely surviving.

Go with a referral from someone you can trust. Check references and go with the best. You are the average of the five people you hang out with, so you want to make sure that you are trading up.

Be especially cautious of the coaching profession. Many of them take an eight-weekend course, sometimes through correspondence, and then want to charge you $250.00 per hour when they have no real life business experience whatsoever. The coaching profession has been marketed to them as a quick way to make $100.00 or $200.00 per hour and they have all bought into the hype. You are officially warned that you must be cautious and make sure a coach or mentor you pay your money to will bring the results you are looking for.

Now, before the coaching pros and universities set a lynch mob on me, let me clarify. I believe in being coached wholeheartedly, but I am also fussy about what experience they have and whether or not they are really going to give the client the real world experience that will help them move their business forward.

BE MENTORED BY A MILLIONAIRE

One of the first truths I learned as a young nineteen year-old from one of the only jobs I ever held was this: successful people are usually very helpful to anyone who wants to hear their story on how they became successful.

I remember that at one of the only jobs I ever had, a large book printing company, the boss was extremely rich. If I had listened to 98% of the people in the production warehouse I would have believed him to be a snobby miserable person who had no time for anyone. Well, I didn't listen to them and actually asked to talk to him, and eventually got to know him. He was a gold mine of information and was willing to help me in any way he could. The production warehouse employees were blind and had their own attitudes mirrored back to them.

There are all sorts of business groups from the Chamber of Commerce, to breakfast business meetings, to associations where you can start getting contacts for a referral. Another really good source is through the Internet, but be sure to check your mentor out thoroughly.

The nice thing about the times we live in is that it is almost free to call anywhere in the world by phone or though your internet connection with companies like Skype. This gives us access and the convenience to speak with people all over the globe. The chances that you could end up with someone who can help you, mentor you, and coach you are better than 100%. That's pretty good odds in my book.

Go with someone who is truly running a successful business or at least has been successful in business. Someone who has not been successful in business can only teach you theory, and in many cases that will just not be enough. Road sense or street smarts cannot be found in a book, so you must have that as a prerequisite to finding a great mentor.

There is a ton of help out there and most successful people like to help. That is why they are successful in the first place. If you help enough people get what they want, you will get what you want. There is no reason on earth that you will not be able to find a multitude of people that will want to help you.

Even saying you don't have time is just an excuse.

"Time is a created thing. To say 'I don't have time,' is like saying, 'I don't want to.'"

—*Lao-Tzu*

If you have a hard time finding a mentor, email me at info@servicebusinessriches.com. You have no place to hide. The secret is out. This is not rocket science. You only need to be open to new information and you will find that your life will be filled with happiness, wealth, health, and unlimited success.

WHY 95% OF US ARE FLAT BROKE AND WHY YOU WON'T BE

I repeat, this is not theory, these are strategies proven time and again by millions of people who have become wealthy and wise by becoming more conscious and aware that doing things in a certain way will bring you success beyond your wildest dreams.

Most of our society has become victims of multi-generational thinking that is keeping them imprisoned at their own will. We have been brought up with beliefs that are not moving us forward to a life of prosperity.

Self-limiting thoughts include those like, "It takes money to make money," or, "You can't have your cake and eat it, too." These are just plain wrong statements. Get rid of these beliefs and replace them with empowering ones.

I think one that is perpetuated the most in our society and gets people really irate when I bring it up is this:

"You have to work hard and be honest to make a lot of money."

I know some of you are already saying that you think I am a little off on this one and are actually irritated by this remark. I have had people say that the above statement evokes considerable emotion if they think they have to give up this belief.

Although I am not against hard work, it definitely does not mean you will become rich doing it. If this were the case, than ditch diggers would be rich. As you know, this is not the case, and a lot of our hardest working people are not rich. In fact, I have seen many people, including myself, actually sabotage their wealth accumulation because they think that they aren't working hard enough to make all the money they want, and therefore, something must be wrong.

Hard work can also be the cause for unbalance in life because some people believe they have to struggle for everything they have in life and that can put unnecessary strain on a family.

When I first started making a lot of money from home just sitting at my computer and talking on the phone, I felt guilty. I would say that it couldn't be this easy and kept waiting for something to happen that would screw it up. It was not until I read about Warren Buffet, the second richest man in the world's daily routine, that I gave up the thought. If it was OK for him, then it was OK for me.

If I had not given up that belief I would have screwed it all up by going back to struggling. I realize now that I am open and more aware and that most of the time I made big advances in business and in wealth they came really easy. In fact, many times it was almost like I made no effort and they just came to me.

The second part of the above quote, "you have to be honest," is misleading. I believe honesty is the only way to live a healthy life, but it does not mean that it will make you rich. You get rich by doing things a certain way and that way is available to us all.

I highly recommend that you read a book written in 1912 by Wallace Wattles called "The Science Of Getting Rich." You can get a free copy at: http://www.scienceofgettingrich. net/

The reason why most people are flat broke when they retire is because they live their whole life with the information that was put into them as kids and they never wake up as adults and obtain new information that will get them to where they truly want to be.

I know that because you are reading this book you have an open mind and are committed to a life of prosperity and that you are not going to let that happen to you. Through the help of the right people and by doing things in a certain way you will never retire without any money saved.

Every time you have an ANT (Automatic Negative Thought) you should decide that you are not going to let is stop you. You will replace that thought with a positive thought that will keep moving you towards a life of wealth, health, happiness, and success. Should you have an ANT that you can't seem to replace with a better thought and are becoming convinced it is real and is stopping you from progress, you should have a mentor to call to help you through it. If your mentor can't figure it out, you can always email me.

There is only one reason for you to not succeed and that is if you have given up. It is your choice, but we are all deserving of great things in our lives. You don't help poor people by being poor.

CAN IT REALLY BE THIS EASY?

Yes! Success is a state of mind and you can change your mind at any point you decide to. It doesn't matter what happened in the past it only matters what you are doing and thinking this very second that will create the future you desire.

Once you have your mindset straightened out you can be, do, or have anything you desire. You are now poised to take the information in this book and explode your business through powerful marketing principles and strategies that will fill your pockets fast with cash like you have never experienced before. You will also discover that with each win and bit of success you will be pushed on to even greater heights and wonder why you hadn't started this journey much earlier.

You must be sure to never go back to your old stinking thinking habits and guard against the dream robbers and naysayer's. You must surround yourself with positive people who support you and keep away from anyone trying to rob you of your dream. As you change your thoughts to wealth, health and success in a habitual way, you will find that you will automatically attract people of similar thinking. This will round out all of the opportunities and abundance in your life and you will never look back.

It is no harder for the likes of Donald Trump, Larry King, and Oprah Winfrey, to do their jobs than it is for others. The difference is they are being, doing, and thinking the thoughts that get them a better result in life then most. I would venture to say that they have an easier job than many people that earn a fraction of the amount that they do.

Many people sabotage themselves by thinking they have to work extremely hard to get ahead and consistently turn away from great opportunities because they think it is too good to be true and don't deserve it.

Some of my biggest leaps in financial gain came not as result of hard work, but rather by being open to opportunities and recognizing them when they came up. I have had many examples of diamonds appearing at my feet. All it took was recognition and acceptance.

Chapter 3

How Do You Get There From Here?

IF YOU FAIL TO PLAN, YOU PLAN TO FAIL

I have never in my life seen one friend, relative, or business associate take a long driving trip without using a map. It is so obvious and yet when people start a business at least 95% have no business plan.

If you don't have a road map the chance of getting lost is high. If you don't have a business plan the chance of failing is also high. What could be more obvious? If you fail to plan than you plan to fail.

There is magic in writing down your plans. Once you put your thoughts on paper, the whole universe will conspire to bring people, circumstances, and events that will magically help you reach your goal.

Many years ago, I learned the power of writing down my goals on paper. I had written out about five financial goals I would like to reach in about a two-year period. I had written them out and not reread them for a couple of years. I was in a bank signing some papers for a truck lease for one of my companies when I suddenly realized I had reached the written goals.

I was required to supply financial information for the lease and it was through this process that reminded me of what I had written down. I was very happy to realize I had accomplished them. Your subconscious mind will seek out and undertake whatever information you have programmed into it. This is why it is so important to be aware or conscious of all the thoughts you are programming yourself with because they will eventually manifest into the real world.

This is a universal law that is as powerful as the law of gravity. It's "What you think you will become." You cannot be happy and sad at the same time, nor will you be laughing and have an angry thought simultaneously. When you are angry, you attract anger and when you are happy you attract happiness. Your inner world is mirrored back to you from the outside world. Understanding this simple concept makes life really easy. You only need to focus on the thoughts of the life you want and with cheerful expectation, and an absolute understanding, you will manifest whatever it is you desire, "guaranteed."

Our present thoughts create our future reality. You create in the present. The present is the only time we live in. We can't change our history and besides that our history's memory of any event is only our opinion of what happened. We can't live in the future so we only have our present. This is our point of power.

Henry Ford said almost one hundred years ago, "Whether you think you can or you can't you are right'.' You can if you think you can. We all have a special gift but unfortunately our biggest problem is that most of us resist it our entire lives. I know this is almost a cliché but if I can make it and am successful, and I mean this in the most humble and sincere way, than anyone can be successful.

You have no excuse not to become wildly successful if you are reading this book up to this point. You have the contact and resources through me and many other places to get the information to become aware of how to be truly healthy, wealthy, and successful. The only reason you are not successful is if you have made a conscious choice to not be.

It really is that easy and once you make a plan and put your goals down in writing, you will have no other option but to become healthy, wealthy, and successful.

BOY THAT SOUNDS LIKE A GOOD IDEA. NOT!

I have seen pain and I have seen more pain. Although I don't like to admit it, I have had some pretty painful experiences in my own entrepreneurial journey. The worst part about what I have just said is that you don't have to go through this pain if you have some information.

The pain I am referring to results from getting into any business that you have not done your homework on in advance. You run the chance of ending up in a business you don't like, doing things you don't enjoy, and worst of all, making no money. How many employees look at the boss as the one who makes all of the money and decide to go into business for themselves, not realizing what they are getting into? If they are to follow in their boss' footsteps, there is a 95% chance that the boss experienced pain and frustration, earning little to no money.

Better yet, how about falling in love with a business that you know nothing about but it turns out to be the opposite of what you think it is. I could provide a whole book full of examples of this situation, but for now I will give two of the best examples.

The first one is about people who decide that they want to open up a Bed and Breakfast. The reason that many fall in love with this idea is that they feel they can semi-retire into a larger dream house. Sounds like a good idea, doesn't it? What could be better than semi- retirement and earning your dream house all at the same time?

A documentary followed ten couples with this romantic dream through the first year of operation and it was not a pretty picture.

The Reality: Having guests in your house 24 hours a day, 7 days a week and some that are not always happy campers is a reality. Although most guests are nice you have some who can be very demanding and now they live with you and expect you to serve at their pleasure!

You may have to deal with drunken guests who plug your toilets on a Sunday holiday at 3:00 in the morning after you've had a tough day.

The reality is that the stress of having people you have to serve in your home all the time turned into a nightmare for the nine out of the ten couples within the first year.

The moral of this story is that if you are conscious, open, and take the time to investigate the situation you are opening yourself up to, you will tend to not make time and money consuming mistakes like this.

The second example is a story of mine from many years ago when I set up a girlfriend in the dog grooming business before either of us investigated the details. She loved our little four-legged fury friends, so what could be better than becoming a hairdresser to her favourite pets? If you love animals, what idea could be better?

The Reality: Can you imagine cutting someone's hair only to have him or her bite you, piss, and shit on you, all for the love of the job? This doesn't take into account the fact that some dogs also bark all day long. By the end of the day you find yourself hard of hearing after listening to ten barking dogs in the store all day.

Falling in love with ideas and not addressing the realties of each business plan can be a tragic and costly mistake. This mistake can easily be avoided with a little knowledge.

The two businesses I talked about here can also be very lucrative with proper training and knowledge, but if it is a business you don't enjoy for the reasons mentioned than chances are you will not make it. You will eventually discover that no amount of money will give you the energy to stick with it.

Another pitfall that many entrepreneurs suffer from is "entrepreneurial drift." We have had a standing joke in our office about whom the boss is having lunch with and what business we will be in today. It is sad to say that many of us don't put much research and thought into the business we choose to involve ourselves with.

Find a truly reliable source to help you investigate, research, and save yourself, in some cases, a lifetime of pain, fear, and financial trouble.

There is a yin to this yang in that if you do your research about what business to get into you can have a quicker path to wealth, health, and success. Choosing the proper path or business for you can make a difference of literally millions of dollars.

WHAT DON'T YOU UNDERSTAND?

There is information out there to solve any problem you come up against. When you decide on a business to put your energy into, you first want to check to see if there are actually people who are finding wealth and success in that business.

Be careful here because looks can be deceiving. You must be able to verify that these business people are in fact doing well. There is a tendency in business to align ourselves with fishermen who always seem to catch the biggest fish. We are dreamers with big dreams, so be careful to not wind up in a tough low-paying industry. It doesn't mean you can't make something work that has not been done before. The point is you don't have to. It is much easier to steal and distribute ideas then to reinvent the wheel. I know of many wildly successful business people who are proud of the fact that they did not have to come up with any new ideas or inventions.

There are many coaches that specialize in all sorts of niche industries that can help you see a clear picture of your business. There are off-the-shelf products available that will save you decades of work if you don't want to try and figure it out all yourself.

I have had business people tell me that their industry is very competitive and that it is hard to get people to buy their products. They can't set sales appointments because it is so competitive and the profit margin in their segment is small and that is just the way it is. Because of their mindset, they become stuck in a self–created trap.

A good mentor or coach can quickly break down those beliefs, and with a few small changes, get the ship sailing again. I have seen people trap themselves within their own mindset time and time again, and all they have to do is be open to new information that can help turn the situation around.

I, too, have been victim of these self-imposed mindsets. I had twenty-six carpet cleaning locations across Canada and was in and out of airplanes like cars. I worked hard and after I sold my business in the mid-eighties, I told myself that I loved making the money but I never wanted to work that hard again.

I had convinced myself that to make that amount of money I would have to work really hard, and because I didn't want to work that hard anymore I was doomed to a life of mediocre income. I know it sounds ridiculous now but when you're in the middle of it, you believe it.

I wasted many years with that ridiculous belief and within that self-imposed financial prison. A good coach or mentor could have pointed out how stupid I was being and then help to create a more positive and successful belief.

As soon as I realized that I did not have to work that hard to make a lot of money, I began looking at opportunities that would suit me better and make a lot of money.

My business partner and I went to a seminar called "The Millionaire Course" by Marc Allen. The course teaches you how to become a millionaire by only working twenty hours a week. We joked with Marc and at the seminar that we came to the seminar so we could learn how to increase our working hours by ten hours a week so we would be working twenty hours per week.

This really shows you how your mindset and how you look at things can make all the difference for you on your path to success. With this being said, I wake up at 5:00 AM each day and go until 5:00 PM or later. The big difference here is that I enjoy what I do so much that it is as if I don't work at all any more.

There are no more excuses because now you know that what you don't know and where you can seek it out in order to save years of frustration otherwise locked in a learning curve.

LISTEN UP! WHAT ARE YOU…STUPID?

I think most of us have heard that the reason that we have two ears and one mouth is so we can listen twice as much as we speak. You must be willing to unlearn in order to let the new information in.

A glass that is completely full of water has no room for any more water. It is the same with our minds. If you listen with an open or beginner's mindset you are now ready to accept new information that can be life-changing. You are not processing the new information with your old mindset but rather processing new information with a beginner's mindset.

Have you told yourself that you finally heard it? Another way of putting it is, when the student is ready the teacher appears. Many people don't listen to what is being said but rather use the time while listening to others for figuring out what to say next. The information is out there waiting for you but you have to listen to it.

"The most important thing in communication is to hear what isn't being said."
                                              —*Peter F. Drucker*

There are mentors and coaches in any market segment that will help you to become the best in you field. You only have to ask good questions and spend twice as much time listening. How do I know that there are so many people out there to help you?

It's simple- there is a universal law that states you get back what you give. As Zig Ziglar points out, if you help enough people get what they want you will get what you want. It is a fact that most people become successful by helping others. The people in this world that make the most money just happen to be the people that supply the most value.

Once you tap into all the people who are aware of this universal law all you have to do is listen and then take action.

Chapter 4

Your Most Valuable Asset That Nobody Knows About

QUIT BEING A MORON

Talk to any successful direct response marketer and ask what their most valuable asset is, and you will get a 100% unanimous answer. These marketers will all tell you that they could lose everything in a fire and have it all back again usually in less than a year, as long as they have their most valuable asset.

A nice thing about this most valuable asset is the fact that it is impossible to lose it if it is stored correctly. In fact, probably the only way to lose it, would be for a complete nuclear war to occur where no one is left behind. Only then would this valuable asset be lost, and even then, probably not for all eternity.

You must be excited to find out what this valuable asset is. Are you frothing at the mouth yet? By the way, did I tell you that most likely 99% of all companies small and large don't keep track of this valuable asset?

All right already! I'll tell you what it is. It is (drum roll, please) your *Customer List.* It is an asset that keeps building year after year and if treated properly, will keep you in the money forever or maybe even longer.

Trucks, office buildings, furniture, and even employees can be replaced and usually very quickly but your customer list is priceless and no one is building, maintaining, or caring for this most valuable asset.

Quit being a moron and start to focus on your customer list. Remember that what you focus on grows. Just to give you an idea of just how valuable some customer lists are, I will give two examples.

Bill Glaser who owns the DanKennedy.com information site says that if you have a mailing list of 1,000 people in the information marketing business you have a million-dollar-a-year business. Bill goes on to say that even if you are not a very good information marketer, a customer mailing list of 2,000 contacts is still a million-dollar-a-year business.

Fred Gleeck who has 58,000 contacts in his customer mailing list at the time of this writing says that each customer is worth between ten cents to one dollar per month in revenue. Fred's customer worth is a little lower than Bill's but they are still both amazing.

Knowing that your most valuable asset is your mailing list gives you a giant advantage over your competition. Most marketers that know this will say that you can take everything away from them but leave them their mailing list and they will have it all back again within a year.

(I'm getting so bloody excited about your customer list I think I am going to have a heart attack!)

Every customer that you add to your list gets added to your bottom line and your net worth. Yet, I have seen so many companies that don't keep track of their customers at all.

If you want to test this concept, go to any trade show and hand out your business cards to people in the booths. A month after the trade show you will find that almost no one will follow up with you. It is totally amazing but it is also the truth.

You will notice that the companies that do follow up are almost always the most successful ones in their industry. Is that coincidence? I will tell you later why most companies don't follow up and why it is not going to happen to you. I am also going to show you that once you truly become aware of how powerful this concept is, you will want a system to build your list each and every day.

Think about this. If you knew, for example, that 1,000 customers might be worth a million dollars a year to you would you not want to build it up to 10 million and then 20 million? If not, close this book now and go back to watching TV.

'COMPOUND CUSTOMERS' THE 9TH WONDER OF THE WORLD

As you probably remember from your days in high school, you learned all about the Seven Wonders of the World. In more modern times, some of our great thinkers deemed that the "8th Wonder of the World" was compound interest. It was deemed a world wonder because of the way money multiplies in size so quickly by compounding.

An example of this would be if you were to take $10,000.00 and invest it at the age of twenty-one into a high yield mutual fund that earned an 18% return annually. You would have $1,029,665.00 by the time you were forty-one years old. This is a dramatic example of how compound interest works. If all you ever did was beg, borrow, or steal $10,000.00 from a friend or relative or anyone at age twenty, then take that amount and invest in a good mutual fund, you would be a millionaire before your 50th birthday. It is so simple that most of our society just misses this powerful "8th Wonder of the World."

Well, if you missed taking advantage of the "8th Wonder of the World," don't worry or be disappointed because I have one that is even more powerful and you have even more control over the odds working out in your favor. What I am talking about is **Compound Customers**, which is the **"9th Wonder of the World."**

When you are a company that "wows" your customers and you have all of your silver service bullets lined up and ready to help your customers become **<u>Cheerleading Customers</u>**, you will build your customer list in a compounding way. You literally get your customers to do your advertising for you and they get the best service and value of any company they have ever worked with. It is a win/win situation that just keeps on giving.

Most companies do not have the faith to give this **"9th Wonder of the World"** enough time to develop. Approximately 90% of companies will not even bother to train their employees to "wow" their customers, or **exceed their customer expectations**. Another 8% of companies try a little bit of **exceeding customer expectations** but do not have the faith to give it enough time for it to develop into the **"9th Wonder of the World."** Let me explain that you must "wow" your customers and **exceed their expectations**. Keep the faith and miracles will happen in your business, **GUARANTEED, 100%**, every time. In your home service business, having faith and **exceeding customer expectations** is a heavyweight marketing strategy that will explode sales.

There are more and more companies who actually stop advertising all together and put that money into training their employees in order to offer the best customer experience possible. Of course, once this happens to customers they become your unpaid salespeople. They win because of the better customer experience and you win because you attract even more customers like magnets.

So now you are ready to do your fishing, planting, and sowing. Each day you are fishing for a few new customers that you can plant and sow into your customer service magic garden. Each customer has the possibility of any number of options, but the neat thing is there is no down side. (I have to calm down now, as I am starting to get too excited!)

The worst-case scenario would be that your customer has no friends but you will have them as a customer for life because that is your intention. The best-case scenario offers limitless possibilities:

- The customer belongs to an organization that has 2,000 members that would love to have a company like yours doing all the work for their members.
- The customer comes from a large family of 75 close relatives that always use the services that she/he recommends.
- The customer is moving his home and business and you earn business from each transaction.
- The customer has been waiting all her life to work with a company like yours and gives you a $500.00 tip.
- The customer has contact with Oprah Winfrey and wants to do a story on the best customer service companies out there, and because of your exposure on her show you end up with 5,000 new customers.

All of this translates into you growing and building your customer list. (I can't take it anymore I have to go lie down now…That's better, now let's carry on!)

As exciting as this sounds, I have not brought into the compounding part of the equation yet. This is all base level initial investment into Compound Customers. The limitless possibilities of the above customer examples exist by generating new customers that offer the same limitless possibilities. I don't know how to calculate how big your organization could grow because it is limitless.

With the **"8th Wonder of the World'** it is simple math. With the **"9th Wonder of the World,** all that you have to do is apply is the best customer service and experience and it will grow exponentially. One customer can mean ten or even hundreds of new customers. When you really think about it, this is why most companies don't make it in the end. They turn off one customer with substandard or poor customer service and this experience can clog a channel of hundreds of customers. Before they know it, they have no one in town that really wants to do business with them anymore.

When you impress or "wow" a customer, they will tell at least three new people, on average. On the other hand, if you do one small thing that a customer is not happy about, and you don't rectify the situation to their satisfaction, you can quickly turn off twenty-four potential customers. This is an average of how many people an unsatisfied customers will tell about their experience with your company if they are not happy. Multiply the compounding effect and you can wipe out a large city's worth of prospects rather quickly. That just doesn't sound like a lot of fun but it happens quite often. It is usually camouflaged by ex-business owners whining with comments claiming that it is a cutthroat business, or that all customers expect is the cheapest price.

While these stupid and broke village idiots are singing their victim songs, other companies are tallying up huge successes. It is your obligation to become one of the wealthy, healthy, and successful ones.

Just focusing on "wowing" your customers and creating **Customer Cheerleaders** will bring you truly miraculous returns. I have seen small companies go from $200,000.00 per year to $3,000,000.00 in a short amount of time just working with this powerful strategy.

"All as it takes is the **_faith_** to keep **_Exceeding Customers Expectations._**"

Bob Burnham

Large revenue increases like those that I just mentioned do not include how quickly your customer list will grow.

THEY FIGHT OVER FIVE DOLLARS

Bowl me over and say good night, but I have seen it with my own eyes. There are businesses that write a customer off for a five-dollar discrepancy. I saw it once in a child's clothing store where the clerk remained adamant that they would not refund $5.00 because of store policy. I can almost guarantee that within five years any service business or retail store with that mentality will be out of business if they don't change policies and treat their customers like the most important people on earth.

When you really think about it, what this store is saying to its customers is that they don't think their customers are even worth $5.00. That just can't be good energy to spread out into your business community.

There are three very important reasons that you should never do this for almost any amount of dollar discrepancy in your home service business.

One: If you think of the *lifetime value of a customer*, it really puts your customer in a different light. I have been in the carpet cleaning industry for many years and the last time I calculated that number it was $34,800.00. This figure was calculated several years ago and using an average transaction of $250.00. This figure takes into account such things as repeat business and referrals.

The nice thing about looking at the lifetime value of a customer is that now you will look at each customer as pure gold. It becomes worth it if you even have to give $5,000.00 refunds that have nothing to do with you because you just want **Cheerleading Customers** for life. When you maintain the attitude of doing whatever it takes to make your customers happy, your word of mouth advertising starts to soar.

Two: Every customer that conducts business with you has the possibility of being an unpaid cheerleading sales rep. Your best customers will always come from referrals. It is always more believable when a customer tells you that you operate a great company rather than you telling customers what a great company you have.

Referral customers are usually less price sensitive and you save on the acquisition costs. They are also easier to deal with because their friends have already pre-qualified them. Most referral customers will in fact spend more money with you the first time because there is already trust established with your company.

Three: Customers that have bought from you once are three times more likely to buy from you again. They are just plain easier to sell to than to a new customer. With today's cost to acquire new customers, it is much more efficient and less expensive to keep the customers that you have happy.

You are sitting on a gold mine and all as you have to do is change your perspective a little bit to see it. Challenge every thought and belief that you have and your life and sales with change dramatically.

AUTO PILOT RICHES

Now that you realize how valuable each and every customer is and that they are all part of your most valuable asset, your customer list will continue to grow. Every customer that you add to the list is like a long-term deposit that compounds each and every year.

When you have this list, you want to treat it well and continue to grow it. The more often you are in contact with the list members, the more likely they are to buy from you again. Frequency or repetitiveness breeds trust, and trusting customers buy more often and spend more overall.

There are many ways to keep in contact with your list and I could write a whole book on this subject alone. For now, I will list a few that you can implement. If you want to learn more ways on how to do this, contact me at info@ servicebusinessriches.com.

It is recommended for most businesses that you touch base through one form or another around twelve to eighteen times per year. Some companies who understand the power of keeping in touch with their customers contact them fifty-two times per year, and some even as frequently as every day. If done properly, your customers will love you and think that they know you personally. This is the goal, a good and solid relationship with your customers.

There are many ways to keep in contact with customers, including:

- Newsletters
- Email
- Ezines
- Birthday cards
- Christmas cards
- Thanksgiving cards
- Voice broadcast
- Fax broadcast
- Announcements
- Sales
- Letters
- Post cards

Bill Glazer of Gage Menswear contacts his customers over fifty times per year with a variety of imaginative and creative sales pitches and promotions, creating many opportunities to stay in the minds of his customers. Needless to say, his is one of the most successful men's clothing stores in the United States.

As you start to set up a system to stay in touch with your customers you will have people entering your sales pipeline at different times. Each customer sale creates a sequence that will vary for each person purchasing from your company.

Once someone has bought your service, you don't want him or her to receive the same selling sequence as someone who has not purchased from you yet. Keeping track of all the different customer contact sequences can become a nightmare, especially if you have several thousand customers.

This is a very good problem to have because there are software programs that can handle all this for you. Once the initial up front work has been done, you can set everything up to run automatically. You can get it to the point that all you have to do is check your bank balance each day to make sure everything is working.

You can fine-tune many aspects of your sequence and increase sales by 2 and 3 times automatically. You can test one sales promotion against another and get almost instant response in your tracking. Once you have it fine-tuned you will want to get as many people into your automated sales pipeline as possible.

There are many different software programs to choose from but I caution you that there are only a few that are worth your consideration. Contact me at info@servicebusinessriches.com and I can direct you to the one that makes the most sense for your business.

Chapter 5

You Like Me, You Really, Really Like Me

THIS SHOULD BE ILLEGAL

In his book, "Influence The Psychology of Persuasion," author Robert B. Cialdini, PHD, talks about the six principles of persuasion and how extremely powerful they are. I recommend this book to every business owner. I will cover each of these principles at various times throughout this book.

Cialdini gives many examples of how powerful these persuasion principles are, and you can see that when the wrong people use them, they can have some very undesirable consequences. He even talks about the Jonestown mass suicide and how these people fell victim to the principles of persuasion.

The fifth principle he talks about is:

The principle of Liking: People like those who like them, whereby two compelling factors reliably increase liking: similarity and praise.

Do you remember the story Sally Field told many years ago during her acceptance speech at the academy awards? She said, "You Like Me, You Really, Really Like Me." People like to be liked and like dealing with people who like them.

One hundred percent of the time you will hear the truly successful entrepreneurs say they love their customers. The unsuccessful ones will be overheard saying a litany of things, such as their customers are hard to deal with, are very cheap, or want everything for free.

It is common sense when you think about it. Do you spend your free time hanging around with people that don't like you? I didn't think so. Of course, you like being around people who like you and enjoy your company.

If you are in a home service business and you don't like your customers, you need to change that attitude fast. You will just not make it in your business if you don't like your customers because they will sense it. It is something that can't be faked; you have to really feel it.

Remember the popular kids back in school that everyone liked? This was because they liked everyone else. If you don't like your customers don't write yourself off quite yet. You merely have to change your perspective and a belief and you will soon be looking for the good in everybody you meet.

Everyone on earth has some redeeming qualities and good points. You just have to be able to see the good points and ignore the rest. The only reason you would not like any of your customers is if you had bought into something that someone else had said which is not your own opinion.

Joe Girard who specialized in using the liking rule to sell Chevrolets became very wealthy using this method. For twelve years straight he won the title of "number one car salesman" by the Guinness Book of World records.

The formula for his great success was very simple. It consisted of offering his customers just two things: a fair price and someone they liked to buy from. And that was all it took, he later claimed in an interview. "Finding the salesman they like, plus the price: put them together and you have a deal."

Get on top of the liking principle of persuasion right away because if you truly want to be healthy, wealthy, and successful, you must like your customers. Anyone can learn and live this principle. Once again, you only have to be open to it and the rest will be history.

Make note that Joe Girard focused on only two things in his sales system and he was the most successful car salesman in the world. When you start putting these marketing principles in this book into action, one at a time you will begin to see miracles you probably never even dreamed of a few months earlier.

THEY EITHER BUY OR DIE

Once you have your lead, you will always want to enter them into your sales pipeline and build a relationship with them by staying in contact. Even add the people that don't buy from you this time. You want to keep adding to your list. Repetitiveness builds trust and trust makes sales. Just because they don't buy from you this time does not mean they won't buy from you in the future. There are many reasons why they may have not bought this time, but your odds are exponentially increased when you stay in contact.

These people are still very good leads and you have paid something to get them this far. They are potential buyers for your home service and it is less expensive to keep in touch with these people than to hunt down new customers.

An example may be that they used another company this time because of price but they were not happy with that company, and because you have stayed in touch with them, you get another chance to work with them.

Take it a step further. Maybe they were happy with the other company they chose, but because the other company did not keep in contact and you did they decide to use you because over time they only remember the company that keeps in contact with them. You can see that either way you can't loose.

If you are sending information or correspondence to your targeted customer there are only two things that can happen over time. They will either buy or die. There are no other outcomes and you will be pleasantly surprised that they will buy because of the relationship you have built with them.

Staying in touch with your customers is a strategy that most companies are not using. I guess that is why 95% of businesses don't make it to their five-year anniversary. Other reasons that businesses choose not to use this strategy include being too lazy or the strategy seems too complicated.

"The fortune is in the follow up."

—Unknown

Neither of the above excuses is valid in our camp because with software the way it is and the fact you could easily sub-contract the process out makes it a certain solution to increase sales. One of the reasons to employ this method is because you are lazy. It really saves you time and money and will increase profits exponentially.

IT'S BECAUSE THEY TRUST YOU

I sometimes hear the victim stories like, "It's who you know," or "They hired the other company because the other company is better known and more trusted." So, how do you get started? Listen up. This is not a negative but rather a positive thing for your company.

People do buy from a person they know and trust and that is a great advantage to you. We were all born not knowing anyone and trust was not something we understood at that point. Trust is something you can establish through the power of your list. By keeping in touch with your customers you will be the one they know and trust. The nice thing is, it can all be done for you through the use of auto responders and software programs.

Building trust is a very easy race to win and your best customers will be the ones who come to you because they trust you. Customers who buy on trust will usually pay a premium to work with your company. Customers who deal with companies they trust are also easier to deal with because they have been pre-qualified.

The other nice thing about building trust through your list is once you have made your first sale with your customer, they are now three times more likely to buy from you again. It just keeps getting better and better.

Customers that hire you because they trust you also tend to refer you to their friends. This strategy accomplishes the very thing that the victim business owners complain about. It makes it hard for your competition to get in because they just don't do this type of marketing. Most will never figure it out even if you tell them. As you tell them about how it works, they in turn will tell you that it will never work and give you many reasons why. You might have to cut them off in the middle of their whining and flood of negativity because you have to take another big deposit to the bank. Don't let the naysayer's ever slow you down on your path to success.

I was on the phone earlier today with a business marketing coach who had telephone-solicited me to sell me on coaching. When people solicit me I am always open to hearing new ideas and sharing mine. I told him about my companies and asked him to share some of his marketing strategies and then I told him mine. To make a long story short he did not employ many of the marketing principles I spoke of but was very impressed. He was extremely impressed with my coaching programs that were generating more money than the ones he was employing. He was also very interested and impressed with my lead generating system. I shared this with him because it attracted customers rather than chasing them away, like he had been doing.

My system was less expensive, more time efficient, and produced a better customer with a significantly higher dollar return. He quickly realized that he could use my strategies more than I could benefit from his. He was blown away and had not heard most of this material before. Did he book his next appointment with me? No. He didn't because he would have to change. He probably thought it was too much work. He went back to earning his average income. That's okay though, because he will now either buy or die when he is put in an auto-responder sequence.

I have to tell you an even funnier story. I was at a marketing seminar just last week in Dallas and in a buffet line with a marketing business coach. He told me briefly about his business and how he was charging an hourly rate for coaching and had a hard time attracting new clients. I quickly told him about a business model that would work very well with his business model and attract more customers that would pay him a better rate. He could also buy the information from a fellow at the seminar we were at for $5,000.00 that would set him up with this system.

Here is the punch line. He told me he could never afford that amount of money and that it was too expensive. This is a guy that is coaching small business owners and he can't afford a $5,000.00 program to increase his business! He was unable to afford a $5,000.00 investment that would make more money for him and his clients. What is wrong with that picture?

The question is, will you have any competition when you implement these strategies? Not in most situations. This is why the rich get richer and the poor get poorer.

HEY AND IT IS EVEN CHEAPER

The economics of keeping in touch with your customers on a regular basis of twelve to sixteen times a year is a no-brainer. I would venture to say that most of your competitors, no matter what segment you're in, concentrate more on getting new customers than staying in touch and mining business from their current customer base. Obtaining new customers is not much of a focus in most market segments.

Obtaining new customers is an expensive process that is quite often not profitable the first time you do business with a new customer. Although you do need a system for bringing new customers into your sales pipeline, if this was the only thing you do, you could eventually put yourself out of business.

Marketing to your existing customers is a much more profitable proposition. First, you are not paying the expensive acquisition cost, and second, they are three times more likely to buy from you a second time.

I really like a quote that comes from Dan Kennedy about this subject.

"Most companies get customers to make a sale. We get a sale to make a customer."

This is a very important mindset we are talking about here. So many companies go broke looking for new customers, yet sitting right in front of them is a diamond mine, their customer list. The list is just sitting there, the company has already paid for it, and they are not using it.

Some companies are even guilty of doing business with their customers and not keeping a database or list. This is the biggest asset a company has and they don't keep track of any customer information. The gold is in the list that they don't keep and the cost is in the acquisition that they go after. This small change in the way you look at and handle your customer list will, in most cases, increase your business 400%.

Please don't let the simplicity of what I have just said fall on deaf ears. The companies that are the true marketing geniuses are executing these simple processes and looking like superstars. This simple process of keeping in touch with your list will fill your pockets fast.

You will learn that the next time you want a vacation or new car, you just have to notify your list about the latest offer, premium or special service you have for them and they will send you the money. As long as you have the best service, your customers will buy, buy, and buy again. Isn't that a beautiful thing?

Chapter 6

Man! It Sounds Way Too Complicated

I HAD TO DO IT BECAUSE I AM SO BLOODY LAZY

I am lazy. Actually, I am really bloody lazy. This is not a problem for me and I am here as an example of a lazy man's way to riches. I used to feel guilty for all the money I would make for just sitting in my basement, reading, typing on the computer, and talking on the phone most of the day.

This was a real problem. I mean, what if someone found out I wasn't really doing anything? It would be terrible. I could lose everything. I could lose my livelihood, money, house, cars, investments, and all the rest. What should I do? I would look for ways to work physically harder but I just didn't like that. I was trapped.

Then, one day I bought some CD's about Warren Buffet who is the second richest man in the world. Maybe if he weren't so lazy, he would be the richest rather than second in line.

The author described his workday as reading, talking on the phone, and then playing bridge at night. My God, I think Warren is lazier than me! Suddenly, I felt all right about what I did, but I also learned the secret that had been behind both Warren's and my success.

Value I know this one is a little overused but it is something you can take to the bank. Warren Buffet's value was that he had created more millionaires than most of the rest of civilized society. His value was what he did for others. And you know when you look at what he has done for so many people he might even be a little under paid.

Value is what I had always given in my businesses. By educating and supplying information that made people richer and with less stress, my work had value for my customers. It is because I am lazy and like to make money that I searched out systems that make money for others in an easy and relaxed manner for the good of all.

I actually start work at 5:00 AM in the morning and quite often finish at 9:00 PM at night. The secret is, I don't consider it work because what I do I enjoy so much that it is like not working at all. I read, write, and let others know how they to can have the life they dream of if they just have the right information and are aware of it.

Being lazy was a blessing and not a curse. It is really the same with any adversity in your life if you can stand back far enough to see a different perspective. Was it not Napoleon Hill of "Think and Grow Rich" fame that said in every adversity there is an equal or greater seed of opportunity? That is the way it has been in my life. You just have to be aware of it.

Take those adversities and turn them into diamond mines. If you are stuck, just email me and I will send out a tow truck.

IT SURE IS A GOOD THING YOU DON'T HAVE TO COME UP WITH ANYTHING NEW

I can hear the naysayers now. Of course there aren't any naysayers reading this book. They are saying "I can't come up with all this great information that I have developed. Bob, you are a genius!" (I like to flatter myself).

Listen, Dummy up! I have not come up with one new idea or concept and I am proud of it. You don't have to reinvent the wheel. The wheels and vehicles are already out there to make you richer than you ever thought possible.

That's it. You are off the hook. Go out and prosper now. I have just eliminated another time-wasting stupid excuse. I say this with complete humility, "If I can do it, anybody can do it."

Is this empowering to you? You don't need to be prettier, funnier, smarter, more honest, or any other self-limiting bull crap belief you have. You can go right now and take any number of off-the-shelf concepts that are currently being used by others to make them very rich.

Why not use concepts that are already working? Not only will you not be walking down a dark alley alone but you will also have a group of people to help you that have been down that road before.

Come on guys, it isn't that hard. The only reason I can see why you are not getting started on improving your existing business is that you know it will work. That's a poor excuse to.

I was at a Bob Proctor seminar in Las Vegas a few months ago and Bob Proctor's seminar called "The Science of Getting Rich" was not invented or written by him, but rather by a fellow who wrote it in 1910. In fact, the author, Wallace D. Wattles, has been dead for over 90 years. This is not new material and it is available to us all. Bob has the rights to this book because it became Public Domain and out of copyright protection decades ago.

Are you hearing me on this one? Bob took something for free that is available to us all and is teaching us about this book and has made tens of millions of dollars doing it. He's not hiding this fact either. He is telling everyone he can. At some points during the seminar he reads this 1910 classic word for word. Isn't that great?

Another great guy, Vic Johnson, at the same seminar told us how he was broke and bankrupt in 1997 living in his friend's car. Not his car, his friend's car because his car had been repossessed. Vic read a book called "As A Man Thinketh" and it totally changed his life. This information is available to us all. He now sells an information product called:

"How I Created a Six-Figure Income Giving Away a Dead Guy's Book"
By Vic Johnson

He took the book "As A Man Thinketh" and started giving it away because it had changed his life. This book is also Public Domain, meaning anybody can take it, and many have.

Vic is very proud of the fact that he doesn't come up with anything new and goes out of his way to tell you. He wants you to know that you can make it. Everything is available to you now; you just have to be open to it.

There are no obstacles only opportunities. Once you realize this it makes you even more daring. For example, my business partner acquired a new specialized work vehicle for his business, and just for fun made the pact that he would never set foot in it. Kind of fun, don't you think?

One of my first business ventures many years ago in the carpet cleaning industry had a fascinating start. The day I opened the business I had never cleaned a carpet. Was that a problem? Definitely not. I hired someone else to clean the carpets. Remember, I'm lazy, especially when it comes to manual labour. I break out into a bad attitude. I think I'm allergic to manual labour.

Don't waste one more minute racking your brain. Just go with what's out there and make a fortune.

SET UP ONCE! SELL FOREVER OR MAYBE LONGER

There are now companies that are using auto-responding systems to build relationships with their customers once the initial customer response is established. Although many companies do not use this type of system to respond to and build customer relations, it is a very good tool and brings success to companies who take the time to set it up.

Automated response systems are being used by direct response marketers, although it can be set up for a home service business just as easily. With this system, you will have a series of automatic follow-up responses to your customer leads. They can be by mail, email, postcards, fax, or even voice broadcasts and newsletters. There are many companies on the Internet that can help with all kinds of features and ways to set up your customers on an auto-responder sequence.

There are so many advantages to setting up an automatic response system through a direct response format that it is a subject one could write a couple of books on. A big advantage is the fact that it can be set up once and used many times over. Any time you do something once and get paid for it over and over is a good thing.

One of the bigger problems most sales organizations have is putting in the effort and labour it takes to make the sales calls plus follow up. I know of some very successful companies that claim it is luck to be able to make a sale without twenty-seven contacts with your customer.

These companies know they will have to make an average of twenty-seven laborious contacts to make a sale. This is a lot of work. Is it worth it? It sure is because these companies are very successful, but unfortunately they are doing it the hard way.

I was also on the phone this morning with a mastermind buddy who was showing me a website that provided information on a business opportunity. The website was okay but that was the least of their problems.

The biggest problem was the fact that the chances of selling a business opportunity merely from a website is pretty much zero with a new visitor. This site had nothing to capture my name or email for follow up.

Had they had some sort of sales name squeeze page they could keep in contact with me and build up a relationship, thus gaining trust. The odds increase dramatically when you keep in contact with the customer.

It could have been as simple a putting in a small submit box that says:

"Get 4 FREE Secret Strategies That Will Make You Rich In The Home Service Business."
> *Please submit your name here.*

Capturing their name and email address could raise your sales by a 1000% and it's automatic.

My buddy and I have checked many websites of this nature and found that there was no one trying to capture names and email addresses. This is a big mistake for these companies. If they are making money without setting up an auto responder, it boggles the mind to think what they could make by keeping in touch with and building trust and relationship with their customers.

The more contacts you have with your customers, the quicker you will build a relationship with them. Customers buy from people they know. You want to position your company in the forefront of the mind of your customers. When you stay in contact with your customers it is like having a fence around them that keeps them in and your competition out.

99% of companies are not very good at following up and building relationships with their customers. This leaves one of the most powerful elements of business building wide open to you and *you will stand out like a rose in a weed garden.*

You will want to set up a system that will contact your customers automatically between twelve and three-hundred sixty-five times per year to build that tight relationship that sets you apart from your competition. This can be done very simply from the first contact through collecting the right information.

Not only can you eliminate the physical follow up work of keeping in contact with each customer, you can eliminate the effort of making the initial contact. This frees up time and energy to put into other areas of your business. There is not only time and energy saved here, but also a lot of money.

When you attract leads instead of going out and chasing them, they tend to be a better quality lead. There is a different sales relationship dynamic that with a little bit of thought it can be easily achieved.

When you have a system in place to attract leads and a system to automatically follow up on them until they either buy or die, you have a very powerful money-manufacturing machine. This may take a little time, thought, and effort in the beginning but it's worth it in the long run and will pay you many dividends.

The big dividend is that once this well-oiled machine is set up it will work for you while you are sleeping or on vacation. You set it up once and will run automatically. Please don't miss the importance of what I have just said because this alone can make the difference between a life of financial struggle and a life of wealth, health, and success.

I have not seen very many businesses that cannot be set up on this system. If you need any encouragement, help, or a referral, please email me at info@servicebusinessriches.com and inquire about auto pilot systems. Because of the success of this system, I field a lot of emails, so allow me at least two weeks time to respond.

SUB IT OUT

Don't fall into the trap of trying to do everything yourself. I have seen too many entrepreneurs fall prey to the trap of saving money only to loose out in the end.

In my carpet cleaning business, I remember the first time we were about to buy a new piece of carpet cleaning equipment for around $10,000.00. It was a cleaning machine that ran off the truck's engine and consisted of a couple of water pumps, a heat exchanger, and a recovery tank. Several employees looked at it and figured out we could build it ourselves for half the price.

Their intentions were good but their economics weren't. Yes, the pumps, heat exchanger, and tanks were cheaper to buy individually, but the knowledge and manufacturing costs were cost prohibitive.

This story always reminds me of the story of the consultant who bought into a large electric generating company in California. One of the generators had broken down and the maintenance people were not able to figure out what the problem was. The company was losing thousands of dollars every day the generator was not working.

The consultant spent about an hour looking at and diagnosing the problem and finally put an X with a magic marker on the part that had to be replaced. This fixed the problem and the plant manager was very happy.

A few weeks latter the consultant sent out a bill for $10,000.00 to fix the problem. The plant manger was very upset with the invoice because he knew it only took the consultant about an hour to do it. The plant manager sent back a letter to the consultant asking him to itemize his bill.

The invoice came back a few weeks later to the manager and it was broken down as follows. To diagnose and find problem was 1 hour of work at $175.00. To know where to put the X to fix the problem and get the plant running again was $9,825.00.

Henry Ford was once questioned by a reporter about how he could run such a big company with such little education.

His response was quick and direct, "Young man, I needn't know much about a lot of things because I can always hire the expertise to do the job properly and efficiently."

You can't expect to be the expert in all facets of your business, so you must be willing to sub out the tasks that require special expertise so that you can better spend your time in the areas that will give you a better return. If you keep doing the $25.00 per hour jobs you will keep making

$25.00 per hour. You must focus on the jobs in your company that create income and wealth without you working for it on an hourly basis.

Don't be tempted to try to do everything because you think you can do it cheaper. You must always be aware of running your company efficiently but also be aware of the cost incurred because the task was not done properly due to inexperience.

Chapter 7

What's The Matter, Can't You Add?

LIVE BY PRICE, DIE BY PRICE

One reason almost all home service businesses start floundering is they don't know what to charge for their services. They automatically lower their prices to attract more customers but it proves to be a formula for financial disaster.

So many companies start with what Michael Gerber calls in his book "The E Myth" an Entrepreneurial Seizure. A technician that is good at what he does decides that the money should come to him rather than go to his boss and that is where it begins.

The technician is making $25.00 per hour and decides that if he goes out on his own he can charge $30.00 per hour and keep all the extra money for himself. The problem is he has no idea how to run or market a business, and even worse, he does no realize that it can cost $75.00 an hour or higher to operate his new business.

More often than not the technician goes broke before he figures out what it takes to run and operate a successful business. For many, the way to attract business quickly is to undercut the competition. In the short term this can work, but in the long term a strategy such as this can spell death.

Some entrepreneurs take several years to figure out they are on a slow death path. They start with all new equipment and then when it is time to upgrade or replace that equipment they don't have the money put aside for it. What they have done is lived on the equity of that equipment and then there is no money to replace it.

By this time, the entrepreneur is so burned out they either get out by choice or they are forced to close shop. This is not a fun situation and is 100% avoidable. The answer is to know what it costs to run your company and make a profit at the same time.

When you know what your numbers need to be to make your business profitable, you will be charging a higher price. This is the next hurdle to cross and is where most businesses fall down flat on their faces. Not all customers will agree with your price and will be unpleasant to you or even down right rude.

If you are the second or third estimate a customer receives and you are a higher price because you are bidding against other clueless companies that wouldn't recognize a profit if it bit them, then they may respond in a drastic way. Although it doesn't happen often, it is a response that most business owners recognize.

The response is:

"Are you crazy?! The other companies offer half of what you charge. What is your problem?"

This response does more damage to more companies than almost any other peril. Most small to medium size businesses think that because of that response they have to sharpen their pencil and bring their prices down to meet the competition, of which 95% of are going out of business anyway.

I am about to give you a **million dollar secret** that almost no one knows about. Even though you will encounter the odd person who freaks out about your price, don't let them dictate what prices you should charge. Never compete on price as a home service business. Those people will break your spirit, break your bank, and put you out of business for their own gain.

The people that are the cheapest will be the fussiest to work with and will be the most disloyal customer you will ever have. Some are also dishonest and I am sorry to say you are being set up because of your lack of awareness.

I know of a few acquaintances and neighbours who will say a fictitiously low price of a competitor that they want you to match. If you fall for their below cost shenanigan you will be broke and stupid before you know it.

These customers will not care once you are gone because there are other companies just as stupid to take your place in the market. These people are few and far in between and you can charge a lot more than you think especially to people who have had to deal with poor quality and bad companies which they found out the hard way could not be trusted.

In the home service business it costs more money to give customers good value, and so the low-balling companies can't afford to give good value for very long.

The secret to charging premium pricing is to offer the best value. If you look, act, and sound like the competition, your customer may wind up going for the lower price. If you stand out from the crowd by looking better, being better, offering better quality and a better experience, you will always attract the best customers. "Wow" your customers by exceeding their expectations.

It is not hard to stand out from the crowd if you follow some of the strategies in this book. Using only a few will bring you better prices, and better prices will change your life. Customers who have had a bad experience will pay you handsomely for your services.

If you are in a home service business and charging a higher price, here are a few ways to stand out from the crowd.

Silver Bullets of a successful service charging higher prices:

- **Late model clean and shiny truck**
- **Professional graphics on truck**
- **Professionally created logo**
- **Professional uniform; preferably a white shirt with logo and name; black tie; black dress pants; clean shiny new shoes**
- **Disposable booties to put on shoes in customer home**
- **Professional business cards printed on good card stock**
- **Scratch pads with logo**
- **Refrigerator magnets; ask to place on fridge**
- **Park on street and not driveway; ask for permission to use driveway**
- **Smile**
- **Don't crowd customer at door; stand three feet back**
- **Brag book with before and after pictures**
- **Shake hands with men only; women should offer hand first**
- **Use their surname as much as possible**
- **In back of mind be saying and thinking nice things about customers**
- **Arrive on time**

- **Thank you cards**
- **Keep in touch postcards**
- **Gift baskets**

You will be absolutely blown away at what some customers are willing to pay a company they can trust.

IT'S A MIRACLE

The miracle of charging higher prices is so powerful that it literally changes your life. Many home service business owner's transition from being broke and stupid to a successful entrepreneur. It is easy to do, you just have to be open to new ideas and take action.

I have worked with many small businesses and one common theme is that they don't have a handle on their financial situation. This would be comparable to driving in the dark with no headlights on. You are an accident waiting to happen and eventually, it will happen. You cannot give good customer service and value to your customers unless you make a profit.

If you don't know if you are making money, you won't know what to charge. I see small business owners all the time complaining they are not making any money and yet they will not take the time to learn their numbers so they can afford to give good service to their customers. There are many small business owners that don't realize how close they are to making a lot of money but stay stupid and broke because they don't know their numbers.

As a business owner, you should have a Profit and Loss statement and a Balance Sheet every month so you can see where you are making your money. This is not an option about whether you should or shouldn't have the statements.

To not have financial statements will cost you more than having them. This was one of the first things my accountant taught me and it has been a blessing.

Successful entrepreneurs know their numbers and consequently make better than above average profits and are set up to rev up. Once you know your numbers there are little adjustments you can make that will easily increase your profits by 300% or more. To give you an idea about how much a 300% increase in profits is, I want to illustrate the following to you.

Lets say you are working hard at you business putting in a lot of hours weekly. For example, let's say as a small business that you make a net profit of $70,000.00 per year. If you increased your net profits by 300% you would now be making an average of $210,000.00 per year. The living standard between a person making $70,000.00 and a person making $210,000.00 per year in North America is substantially different.

Unfortunately, earning $70,000.00 per year in North America you are just getting by. At $210,000.00 per year you will have the luxury of a nicer home, car, education, vacations, investments, and donations. Doesn't that sound like a much more enjoyable life? You have many more options and you bring up the living standard of all those around you, too. Prosperity creates prosperity.

If you are not making $70,000.00 per year, don't worry. It is more about making a profit you can easily multiply. If you aren't making a profit then it does not matter how many times you multiply it because it will still be zero. That is why it is so important to have financial statements and know your numbers.

When I first talk to new businesses and tell them about increasing their profits they sometimes look at me in disbelief. They tell me I don't understand the market and that a 300% increase in price will just not work. I don't know why I am surprised that more people don't know this little secret and how it can change their life.

You don't have to raise your prices by 300% to increase your profits by 300%. In fact, you may only have to increase your prices 10% to gain a 300% increase in profit. I have shared this secret with many business people and the results are always dramatic and life changing.

Let's say that right know you are making $5.00 profit for every $100.00 in gross sales. If you raised your gross sales dollars by 10% that would translate into $110.00 gross sales and a profit of $15.00. Obviously $15.00 profit is three times the $5.00 profit or a 300% increase. When you raise your prices like this there is no extra expenses involved to do so. It does not cost you any more to charge $110.00 instead of $100.00 and as you can see, the difference on your profits is dramatic.

If you practice all little silver bullets to stand out from the competition, you will find that raising your prices from 10% to 20% is a very easy thing to do. In this example you would actually increase profits by 500% if you raise them 20%. Let me say again that you will increase your profits or paycheck by 500% by only raising you prices by 20%. If we take that same $70,000.000 from earlier you will now be earning $350,000.00 per year.

In my company we notice that with the "wow" factors alone we find we can charge a substantially higher price and receive substantially higher tips. Have you ever received a $500.00 tip for your work? We have had this kind of response from our customers over and over again. Take your company to the next level and raise yourself above the competition.

We can take this a step further by beginning to focus on the processes or areas of your business that are the most profitable. You will probably find that like most businesses I have worked with, 80% of your profits come from 20% of your work. If you can eliminate the 80% of the non-profitable work from you're routine, this will give you 80% more time to focus on the 20% that is profitable.

If you filled that additional time with four times more of the 20% that has been profitable, you could now be earning 1.4 million dollars per year. Remember that what you focus on grows, so when you start to focus on your profitable areas and increase your per sale price, a nice profit is exactly what you will get.

Only your thinking sets the limits so don't limit yourself by not thinking big enough. This is really only the tip of the iceberg and if you want to learn more ways to increase your profits, just email me. I will tell you about additional ways that translate quickly into dramatic results.

I THOUGHT ONLY BRAIN SURGEONS MADE $500.00 PER HOUR

When you really begin to focus on the areas of your home service business that are profitable and focus on making those processes even more profitable, you will quickly see you have the ability to earn $500.00 per hour.

The hourly rate that can be earned in many home service businesses by focusing on the right areas and processes is often more than some surgeons make. This is not the norm in most businesses but it is possible for almost any business to produce these kinds of numbers.

You will also find that the more you focus on profit areas and increasing your profits, the more your profits will increase. The old saying that success breeds success has quite definitely been my experience and it can be yours, too. Involve others in your organization with the same mindset and you will explode your profits.

The more people that focus on this principal, the more opportunities and situations they will attract that offer greater possibilities. As you climb to the next level, you will have an even clearer view of what lies beyond.

I MAKE ALL THIS MONEY FOR ONE LITTLE CHANGE?

Continually keep looking for and utilizing small changes or silver bullets that can change your business. A small change in ad copy can bring you big dividends. It could be the way you state your guarantee or it could be your testimonials. When you work with a good business mentor or coach you will see these ideas start to work for you.

Once you have heard or seen a good mentor or coach come up with some real winners for you, it will start to plant seeds in your mind to come up with your own blockbuster ideas and changes. Little changes, like collecting the names of prospective customers and staying in touch with them via email, auto responders, or mailing sequences, can increase your business substantially. Most companies do not follow up with prospective buyers.

Some new home service businesses only win one out of three quotes or estimates. These potential customers become the target market. Putting their name into a sales pipeline can in many cases double sales. This little effort can deliver really big results. Sound like too much work? Don't worry because you can sub your follow up out.

Remember, once the system is set up, it keeps going bringing in responses requiring no additional work on your part. It is a lot more work to not keep in touch with your customers than it is to set up an auto responder system that does the work for you. I know I am harping on this one but it works so well and so few choose to do it.

A small name squeeze page on your website can be an ongoing way to build your customer list. If you offer them something for free, your will give you their name and email address providing you with a resource for obtaining new customers. Go to http://www.servicebusinessriches.com/ for an example of a name_squeeze page. Enter your name and email address and you will experience automated follow up.

These customers get some really great information for free and you get to stay in contact with them. There is a double whammy with this one that includes the "law of reciprocity" that works in your favour when you use this approach. We will cover this later in this book.

You can build your customer list very inexpensively through eBay. Find something you can put up for sale on eBay that your target market would want to buy. You may even want to sell at a very low price to gain a customer. Through eBay they are now added to your sales pipeline and you keep in touch with them through auto responder sequences. Think of the customer list you can build by selling on eBay.

The list of things you can do for free to build your company list with qualified targeted leads is endless. You just have to learn them and implement them. If you add all these things together you will really be making some good money.

How do you discover all of these things that you can use in your business? You can go to mentors and coaches that have those types of information, attend seminars and home study courses, and listen to CD's and cassettes. I need to caution you that I am talking about outside-of-the-box ways of doing business and finding the people that know these strategies may be difficult, but they are out there.

I have contact with people who understand these strategies and, as always, you can email me for a referral at info@ servicebusinessriches.com. Please be fussy in who you use and make sure they are a reliable referral that will dramatically change the way you do business. This type of marketing can cut decades off of your learning curve.

There is a lot of bad information out there that can keep you spinning your wheels for a long time. I like to point out how many people I have seen in business with one year's worth of experience twenty-five times over. You want the mentor with twenty-five years worth of kick butt strategies that will put you ahead by twenty-five years in one year's time. The good information is out there and it can be found being utilized by the truly successful people.

Chapter 8

I Almost Messed My Pants! I Met A Guru

YOU'RE LOOKING AT ME DIFFERENT. DO I HAVE PEPPER IN MY TEETH?

I am going to tell you one of the most powerful ways to attract customers that are pre-qualified and will pay you a maximum dollar for your services. Almost no one is using this powerful strategy, and in some cases where it is being used, the people don't understand how this strategy has improved their sales and life.

I want to start by telling you that in our society in North America we pay a higher premium to work with and get advice from people that we perceive as EXPERTS. This is a fact.

Another principle in his book, "Influence: The Psychology of Persuasion," author Robert B. Cialdini, PHD, talks about "Authority."

The principle of Authority: People defer to experts.
People seek out and pay premium dollars to people who they perceive to be the expert. Here is the kicker. There is no board that certifies and appoints experts. Many business people say that they are not experts. This is not true when you really think about it.

No matter what business they are in they have more knowledge about that business area than their customers do, making them the experts. You customer wouldn't have called your company if they didn't think you were good at what you did.

Business people are often hesitant to label themselves as experts. They are afraid to play bigger because they believe they are not yet qualified. They're waiting for something to happen - a certification, a degree, a blessing from the gods in their industry, or a diploma to certify "Expert hood" from their respected peers.

Expert status doesn't happen this way and so many business people have not figured this out. The only one who really has the capacity to declare themselves an expert is you. Do it now and don't wait one more second.

Experts have more credibility, are more respected, easily get media attention, can market more easily and inexpensively, are paid more, and receive less price resistance. Don't wait for someone to invite you into the expert club. Appoint yourself now by walking past all the people at the back of the room.

The silver bullet and fastest way to becoming the expert is for you to **Write a book**. Once you have written a book, you instantly obtain expert status and leapfrog to the front of the room. People will look at you differently and have more respect for you. It almost sounds a little crazy and doesn't even make sense, but in North America once you have written a book you are regarded more highly.

Like it or not, when you become the author of a book, you also become a celebrity. You get all the natural benefits that go with celebrity status. Your world changes from chasing a dollar to dollars chasing you if you promote your book properly.

You don't have to question why, you just have to welcome all the opportunities that come along with your newfound fame. It is something to be enjoyed and to be utilized for the good of all. Once you have this status you will enjoy a road less travelled.

Now before I go any further with this claim, I want to talk to the people whose eyes are currently glazing over. You are the ones that were with me when I first mentioned becoming an expert, gaining credibility and fame, and earning more money, but then went sideways when I said that writing a book guarantees this.

This is the part where some people are lost because they claim they can't write a book. Some have even tried for many years and still have not been able to do it. Others will say they just don't have anything to write about. I don't want to seem flippant but if you are breathing right now, you have what it takes to write a book.

If you can speak conversational English, I assure you that you can write a book and don't let anyone tell you anything different. Not only can you write a book, you can, with the right information, write it very quickly and make it so people can't put your book down until they are finished reading it.

Writing a book is obtainable by everyone. You just need the right format to write with and success is assured. In North America, approximately 81% of our population want to write a book but they just don't know how to do it. With the right information and structure there are novice writers who are able to write a book with ninety pages or more in several days on their first try.

Don't reinvent the wheel when writing your book. There are many people out there that can help you quickly and inexpensively get the job done. There are several books and ebooks that you can buy though bookstores or online that teach you the many ins and outs of writing your own book quickly and easily. I also recommend http://www.Expert-AuthorPublishing.com. I have done all the hard work and I want you to take advantage of it. We can show you or even do it for you and you reap the benefit.

If you choose to not write a book after hearing about the benefits, it is because you don't want to and not because you can't. There are no excuses that can't be quickly overcome. I must repeat this last statement because it is so important. There are no excuses for not writing your own book that can't be quickly overcome. It is much easier than you think with the proper help and direction. If you get stuck, go to info@servicebusinessriches.com and I will send out a tow truck.

The new leads that writing a book will generate for your business will knock you over and you will wonder why you struggled so hard for so many years. You will be included in circles of people you had not had access to before and it will benefit you immensely.

There is one very important point about writing a book that I just had to save to the end. It is the icing on the cake and will be the biggest long-term benefit to you. Once you have a published book, your confidence will soar.

One of my favourite quotes is:

"Money is an idea backed by confidence."

You will have plenty of confidence as a by-product from writing your book and you will have plenty of money, too. Don't hesitate. Get started as soon as you finish my book and your whole world will miraculously change. I can personally guarantee it from experience.

I CAN'T WRITE A BOOK. WHAT ARE YOU CRAZY?

Because this will be one point that will float around in your consciousness, I want to address a few more points before moving on from this challenge of writing your own book. Because this is one thing that will have dramatic impact on your life, I want to make sure you are up for it by addressing a few questions.

Many people think they can't write a book because they either failed or almost failed English. You will find that a conversational style of book writing will be more popular than a more grammatically correct book. If you can hold a conversation you can write a book.

Some people will say it is just too intimidating or overwhelming and, where do you start? Start buy getting good information on how to do it through the Internet, referral, or just send me an email. There are tricks and tips that make the process quick and easy.

I just can't write and that is all there is to it. Even if you just can't write you can come up with an idea for a book and work with a ghostwriter who will help you write or even write it for you. You can go to http://www.elance.com and put your book out for bids and have 20 writers that will bid on writing your book for you. You can check out their reference and sometimes read other books they have written so you can choose the one you like.

I can't even come up with an idea for a book. This excuse won't work either. If the right coach or mentor asked you the right questions you would have a book idea in a matter of minutes. There just isn't a reason not to write a book. If there are no reasons to not write a book, and many life-changing reasons to write a book, then the answer is clear.

Write your book and do it now. Don't stop until you are done and get mentoring and coaching to keep you going. Once your book is written, please send me a copy and also let me know how it has changed your life. I love to hear from my customers and readers, especially if they have found success.

Get your book in as many hands as possible because books are better than brochures and business cards by a long shot.

And You Want A Number One Best Seller As Well?

There are many ways to market your book and most will not be the traditional way most publishers are doing it. Actually, you will find that most publishers will not market your book at all and it is up to you anyway.

There are even people that will guarantee you that your book will be a number one best seller on amazon.com. How cool is that? This is something that has only been available for a short time but if you have money to do this, it is a guaranteed way to become a bestselling author and even raise your credibility to a higher level. This process even comes with an iron clad money back guarantee. If your book doesn't become a bestseller on amazon.com, you will be given your money back.

Check out the website http://bestsellermentoring.com/. It explains how this system works and how it can work for your book. I can't quote a price for this service but it is not that expensive and the returns can literally change your life.

It is all so easy and fool proof to boot. Just the right knowledge that is available to all of us and we have the path for wealth, heath and success. I see so many people and authors struggle for many years both mentally and financially. If they had this information and made a few very small changes, it would have made a world of difference for them.

The funny thing is, you can help more people by being successful than by being poor, so why not go for it, especially when there has never been a time in history where it is easier to be successful. With all the technology, information, and people who love to help their fellow man, it amazes me why anyone would continue to struggle.

As was discussed in the beginning of this book, we are the sum of our thoughts and if we want a different life, we have to think differently. This book can provide the ideas that can change your life and all as you need to do is take action.

WE'RE SO STUPID! ISN'T IT GREAT?

I'm not smart enough won't work for you either. We can be stupid and I know I have been and I am damn proud of it and still make a ton of money. So why are there so many teachers, doctors, and lawyers that are broke today?

If it took intelligence to make money and be rich, than the university professors would be rich. That is just not the case. In fact, being too intelligent might even prove to be a handicap. Some very intelligent people can over analyze the situation to the point that it paralyzes them from beginning anything.

Some highly intelligent people are very good at coming up with all the reasons why an idea won't work, while other less intelligent people are making ideas work. I have seen this phenomenon in action. In fact, if I had the information that I have today thirty years ago I may have never started. The other side to that coin is people strike it rich doing something that is very simple and that does not require years of schooling.

Once you catch on to how truly easy it is to market your company and make money, it becomes a game that gets to be more fun as time goes by. When you focus on the right area, right marketing, and right business, it is a sure thing to make you a lot of money.

In most cases, it is a matter of unlearning information more than anything else. It is our old ways of habitual thinking that get us in trouble. It is often what we know rather than what we don't know that keeps us imprisoned.

An open beginners mind without any preconceived baggage will carry a person much further quicker. The information that can carry us to great heights is available to us all, but most of us are just not aware of it or we have limiting beliefs and won't let new information in. Be open and prosper and we will all be glad you did.

Chapter 9

I Thought They Arrested People For Stealing

I AM SO PROUD I CAME UP WITH NOTHING

So many people have this crazy limiting belief that they have to come up with something new and innovative to be successful in their business. It's a myth and I am giving you permission here and now that you do not have to come up with anything new, and in fact, I want you to steal each and every one of my ideas.

I want you to steal my ideas because I stole them from someone else and I am damn proud of the great ideas I have stolen. I don't steal the bad ideas, only the ones that truly work. I steal ideas from successful people because they tell me to and I want you to steal from me in return.

I am not talking about stealing property, patents, or copy written material. I am talking about the great marketing and business tips that are available to us all and that can make us wealthy, healthy, and successful.

You see examples of companies taking each other's business marketing ideas all the time. A recent example (at the time of this writing) is the General Motors sale that claimed you could get their cars at employee pricing. Shortly thereafter, both Chrysler and Ford announced the same sale.

Although this sale boosted sales in the short term, it was a very poor marketing idea for the long term. Now GM is in financial trouble. Even big companies don't understand how to market their products and quite often depend on morons to help them out.

If they would go back to basic marketing strategies, such as providing value, superior products, and service, they could turn their situation around. Do you think anyone at GM will listen?

Planet Hollywood restaurants stole an idea already being used by other restaurant chains. The idea of theme restaurants is a solid idea but they forgot a very important marketing piece of the pie and paid dearly for it.

We were in Las Vegas about seven years ago when Planet Hollywood was still going strong. We decided to give it a try. The theme of the restaurant sounded like a great idea.

We ordered our food from a less than pleasant waiter but we still had a smile on our faces. We were on vacation and didn't care. It was only one strike against them and we are forgiving.

We waited an extremely long time for our food to arrive. I mean an extremely long time. But we were hungry and nothing was going to get us down. The food came and even though we had waited and were very hungry, it was not very good.

Still smiling, I thought maybe it was just one of those nights that things weren't working for them. We all have a bad day once in a while, so I still kept that smile on my face.

While all this was happening, we did not have one person ask us how it was going for us or if we were enjoying our meal. I thought for sure that at the front desk on the way out, they would ask how everything was, but that was not the case either, so I decided it was time to approach them and tell them that things were not that great.

I guess you will not be surprised to learn that the hostess was not at all interested in what I had to say and offered no resolution. I have to admit as I was leaving the restaurant I was not smiling and told my wife to mark my words that they would be out of business in one year's time.

I was wrong. It took only six months for them to fall into bankruptcy. I know that they had several consulting companies come in after that to try and turn things around but it did not work. Now you never know whether the owners will cooperate, but if they had cooperated, it could have been very easy to turn it around.

How did I know their future? I could easily tell by their intention. The concept was good. They had some Hollywood heavyweights that owned it, but their intention was not to make the customers happy it was to make money from their gimmicky theme. After you had seen the restaurant once, it needed to be better in other ways to keep the customers coming back. They had no training or infrastructure. The first line of intention always comes from the top and filters all the way through the company. If you don't have the proper intention at the top, it is a dead end.

No great advertising or marketing gimmicks are going to keep you in business if you don't apply one of the most basic ingredients to success. You must always exceed your customer's expectations and blow them away with better than expected value, quality, and service. You can only trick a customer once if you don't follow this basic principle and if you have to get new customers all the time it becomes so cost prohibitive you will ultimately go broke. Simple,

simple, simple, but it still amazes me how many companies don't understand the basics.

This was an obvious mistake for Planet Hollywood and they paid dearly. You can run a business for a short while on gimmicks, price, and other short-term promos, but if you don't have the long-term intention of excellent customer satisfaction, you will not grow as a company or an individual.

If a company does not have a person at or near the top of the organization with good intentions, your company will be in trouble. Don't let this happen to your company. Put in safeguards to make sure your most valuable asset, your customer list, is strong and healthy.

If you see an idea that is working in your industry or another industry that could be adopted by you, by all means use it and make some great money. Just make sure you are not following some poor sheep that is about to jump off the cliff.

GO AHEAD, JUST TAKE IT.

Just take these ideas and implement an idea one at a time. Don't let yourself get overwhelmed with too many ideas. Focus on one and implement it. After you have taken action on your first stolen idea and it is working well, then steal another idea. That's right, just take it and implement. I give you my permission. Of course, start with the ideas in this book and you will be rich before you even have to try anybody else's ideas.

This is not rocket science. Too many business owners complicate the easy to their detriment. I have given people great ideas that will quickly change their financial situation, but they don't take them because they complicate things. Just take them and go for it.

You are better to try and fail and at least have something to improve on than not take the idea and try it in the first place. When you hear a new idea, write it down immediately. This will help to imprint it into your subconscious mind. Your subconscious mind will automatically take action to make it a reality.

Taking one idea and making it work will give you the momentum to get started on implementing the next one. Remember, most good ideas have the power to increase business at least 10 % or more and there will also be ones you take action on that double and triple your profits. Get started and get into the habit of just taking those ideas and going ahead and using them.

IT'S THE PRINCIPLE! I DON'T WANT TO COME UP WITH SOMETHING NEW

I go to seminars and I recommend that others go, too. I know some people who spend over $100,000.00 per year on seminars, CD's, information products, books, and courses. I don't think it is any coincidence that they are usually the ones that are the biggest earners. I spent about $25,000.00 myself last year and plan to increase that amount this year.

This past year in Las Vegas, Bob Proctor had his "Science Of Getting Rich" seminar, which is taken directly from the book of the same name written by Wallace Wattles. It is not something he designed himself as this book was written in 1910. He is the first to tell you he studied it and has probably read it over a thousand times.

The point is this is something he likes, has value, and can help us all and he is bringing it into our awareness and teaching it's wisdom. It is not his idea. Bob is bringing forth someone else's work and because it is good it makes it such a successful seminar.

Another presenter was a fellow that made his money from a website called "As A Man Thinketh." Vic Johnson's material comes from a book that was written by James Allen in the early 1900's and Vic makes it a point in his presentation to tell you all his information is not new and is stolen or borrowed from others. He prides himself on the fact that he doesn't come up with anything new and uses this to illustrate that we all have the same opportunity.

It is almost a principle with Vic that he only uses what is already out there. He really illustrates the point that we can all be successful just like him.

LET YOURSELF OFF THE HOOK, ITS EASIER

Let yourself off the hook of always having to come up with something new. Become an investigator that looks for great information that is already working for someone else and apply it to your own business.

With this approach you will free up so much energy that you will better be able to focus and implement tried, true, and tested ideas. Howard Shultz of Starbucks fame didn't invent coffee and McDonald's Ray Kroc did not invent hamburgers and yet they made hundreds of millions of dollars using these existing ideas.

> *"Ideas are a dime a dozen. It is in the marketing that fortunes are made."*
> —*Bob Burnham*

Shultz and Kroc always remembered the most important laws of marketing and they are to provide value and exceed their customers' expectations. They remember to take these ideas and execute them better than people have done in the past and they remember that it is in the marketing of any idea that the fortunes are made.

You can have the best idea or product in the world, but if you don't know how to market it the business will fail. You can also have some ideas or products that aren't new or exciting but it is in the marketing that makes them so. The Pet Rock is probably a great example of what marketing can do for an idea or product that didn't start with much.

There are not many products that have such a limited appeal and use as the Pet Rock, and yet through marketing it was a great success for a period of time. You can market anything with the right strategy and ad copy but you must have the best service and value to create long-term customers that will keep coming back to you for life.

When you start focusing on ideas that are already out there and working, you will find you have hit a gold mine of material that is waiting for you to implement. Take the available information and ideas and run with them.

Chapter 10

Use The Information In This Book And If It Doesn't Bring Your Business a Thousand Times What You Paid For The Book Within One Year, I Will Give You Double Your Money Back For The Price Of The Book

*%#@**! OR GET OFF THE POT

Rock Solid, Iron Clad, No Risk guarantees for your customers will bring you big increased sales results and, once again, hardly anyone is using them to their advantage. Most companies have no mention of guarantees in their printed material and if they do it is hard to find or is weakly defined.

You will recognize these waste of time guarantees with verbiage such as "Guaranteed to your satisfaction" or "We guarantee you will be happy." What the hell kind of guarantee is that? It doesn't make a statement about you believing in your company, does it?

When I first tell business owners that their guarantee has to be bold like, "Double your money back" or "Guaranteed for life", they start to get gun shy by saying you are going to get customers that will take advantage of you, causing you to lose money.

The truth of the matter is that if your company is giving a large amount of refunds, you may want to check to see if your customers like you, because most customers don't ever ask for their money back. It may be that your customers just don't like the way you are doing something.

You will want to get to the bottom of high return rates immediately because for every one person who is unhappy there are sometimes twelve more people unhappy that won't say anything. This is a large problem you want to have rectified right away.

Once you are sure your company "wows" your customers and you're exceeding customer expectations, you are now ready to attract many new customers by having a guarantee that no customer can resist. The better the guarantee, the more customers will be attracted to your company.

A rock solid guarantee that stands out from the competition can double or even triple your response rate. Will you get more refunds? Some companies may but it will only be a small percentage in comparison to the large increase in business. If you do it right, not only will you not lose, but you will gain financially.

You must always keep track and test the response you are getting from each ad you place. Small changes to some of your words can make huge changes in response. Be careful to change only one thing at a time so you know what is affecting the response.

The type of business you are running will determine the best way to create a killer guarantee. You want your customer to be 100% sure in their mind that you will stand behind your company and that your home service is so good that you communicate a message they can't resist

Here is an example of a guarantee where one brings in a better response with minimal refunds. Some companies will give a 60 and 90-day no-questions-asked refund and will get a good response because of the guarantee. Taking this guarantee even further would be to offer a lifetime guarantee.

There are two reasons you want to do this. First, when you have a lifetime guarantee, you will increase your response rate significantly and often leave your competitors scratching their heads. Second, when you extend it from 30 days to lifetime, the customers are less liable to mark on their calendar that they have to make sure they like your service within the 30-day window.

Have you ever marked a date down about refund policy so you wouldn't forget? I know I sure have. When you offer a lifetime guarantee, they know by your confidence that you believe in your service and because there is no time constraint to mark it down, there is nothing to put down on the calendar. Because they don't put it down on the calendar they tend to forget.

You will find some companies that have some pretty good guarantees but then they nullify that great guarantee by adding various exclusions so you can't receive a refund. They have so many hoops for the customer to jump through that the customer just looks at it with the mindset that they offer such a great guarantee because they know the customer will not be able to get a refund.

These companies cancel out the goodwill of the guarantee by not trusting the customer's action with the service. If you don't trust your customers, then don't give them the guarantee. You will find that when you include a lot of restrictions and hoops for the customer to jump through, you will get a few aggressive customers saying they knew there was a catch.

Put 100% trust into your customer and they will trust you 100%. It should be a no questions asked refund policy. Your customer has to feel good about the transaction. When they do, they will respond in kind by buying in bigger quantities and the number of refunds will hardly increase at all. Have faith in your fellow man and they will have faith in you.

Having faith will bring you into bigger profits and create happy customers. Don't piddle around on this one. If you get off the pot and go for it, you will see miracles happen.

IRON CLAD. YOU TAKE THE RISK

When you have kick butt Iron Clad guarantees you are also solving another hurdle your customer may experience. Many people are very careful with their money and don't like to put it at risk. If they think there is a risk in the transaction they are very leery to give you a try.

By having an Iron Clad, no-questions-asked total-refund-for-life guarantee, you as the business owner assume all of the risk. This risk reversal tactic is a powerful motivator for most consumers. It removes any doubt in their mind and they are able to move forward with confidence in your company.

Risk reversal is so powerful you will wonder why more companies are not using it once you see your results. I read yesterday on the CNN Money website about how three large department stores are tightening there refund policies this Christmas. They say that they get about a 3% return refund rate and that it is too high.

I have to say to the credit of the writer of the article that he saw how stupid these large chains were being. The reporter noted that with the large cost of acquiring customers it is a rather stupid policy that will possibly turn away customers.

If one out of the three stores gave a better Iron Clad guarantee during Christmas and advertised the fact, they could quickly gain a larger market share while the other two department stores were sleeping. It never ceases to amaze me how stupid some of these big companies can be.

Many big companies follow the advice of university trained people that don't really have a clue about real world marketing and end up wasting a lot of their company's money on marketing ideas that just don't work anymore. Don't get me wrong, I am a big believer in higher education and invest substantial amounts annually to educate myself, but in many cases the old school ways are totally obsolete.

Phil Laut, author of "Wealth Without a Job", is a graduate of Harvard Business School and teaches and coaches entrepreneurs all about mindset and marketing techniques they just don't teach at Harvard. His ideas work and if you get into the mindset and follow his coaching, you will be a rich puppy pretty damn quickly. Visit his website, http://www.phillaut.com for more information.

I have seen a company in my industry offer a "double your money back" guarantee. It is a carpet cleaning company and the woman who owns it, who is a great marketer, offers the Iron Clad guarantee that if you are not 100% happy with their cleaning service, they will give you double your money back.

It was interesting when she explained her guarantee to a group of competitors on a teleseminar, and explained how many new customers it produced for her. Even when she pointed out how well it worked, there were mostly naysayer's there that said the customers would wind up taking advantage of them.

The interviewer on the call asked how many refunds she had given to customers and the answer was an amazing, "**NOT ONE.**" You would think that at least a couple of people would have asked for a refund, but in the two-year period that she had been offering it, she had ZERO refunds. Isn't that just great?

She also elaborated on the fact that her sales were increased substantially by giving this Iron Clad no risk double your money back guarantee. And even after that, there were still mostly sceptics.

These guys were arguing for their right to be broke and stupid and I think a few were wearing the Village Idiot cap, too. This stuff works and there are people that will testify about how powerful it is. *(Excuse me, I have to go deposit some money right now. I'll be back it a few minutes).*

I would sub that bank job out, but I still get too much of a kick out of it to let it go. Play with your guarantees and make them stand out from the crowd. You want **BIG BOLD GUARANTEES** and then you'll be counting the cash.

Do You Have The Kahoonas Or Are You Going To Be A Whiny Baby?

Don't be like the whiny babies on the teleseminar that I just spoke of. Test as many guarantees as you can. Grow, test, and develop them. The more confidence your customers have in your company and in your product, the more likely they are to pull out their checkbook.

The same is true for you and your company. The more confident you are that your service or product is the best, then the more you will realize you want to advertise that fact in a big bold way. You cannot be timid in this area of your business because timid actions will bring timid results.

You will notice in some industries how the guarantees evolve over time. You will always want to be out in front of the pack. You know that you can easily be out in front of the pack because the return rates are so low, especially if your service is the best and you do what you say you will do.

The consumer is on your side if you're on his by delivering a great service. It is such a simple formula that is available to all and yet most will not use it. Have faith in the honesty and goodwill of your customers and they will have faith in you.

It's The Law, That's Why

There are laws of nature such as gravity that no one can escape. These are universal laws and there are many such universal laws in business as well. The law of gravity works for us all and leaves no one on the sidelines. There is no one that can opt out.

When you guarantee your service in such a way that leaves no risk to the customer, this makes a very compelling offer because you absorb any risk. It also makes sure that you are confident in what you are selling or else you would not do it.

I have made the title of this book, "How To Make A Million Dollars In Your Home Service Business Guaranteed", because I know with 100 % assurance that if you follow all or some of the strategies in this book, your home service business will bring in gross revenues of over a million dollars per year very easily. This is not a theory. It is something that has been done many times.

If you follow these strategies you will find it difficult to **not** make over a million dollars in gross revenue in your home service business. People who read a guarantee such as this have confidence that they will not be wasting their time or money on this book. If you are confident in your service you should state that in a big bold guarantee so that people will feel it.

Don't be timid because your customers will sense your fear and run the other way. If you are confident that your service is the best, then let your customers know. You will always bring in more sales with a big, bold, confident guarantee and you may even double or triple your response.

You may get a few refunds in some types of home service businesses, but it will be dramatically offset by the increase in response to your ads. Don't let a few refunds spook you. Keep your eyes on the glass being half full and not on the odd cranky customer that did not give you a fair chance because they woke up on the wrong side of the bed that day.

You will that your competition doesn't utilize guarantee strategies because they don't know how powerful they are or are afraid their customers will take advantage of them. This is one silver bullet that will put you ahead of the competition quickly. Just like the law of gravity, the law of big bold guarantees will work well for you.

Play with your guarantees to see which ones attract the biggest response. You will find the one that has the sincerest message to your customer. Push the boundaries of your comfort zone and you will be pleasantly surprised that your customers just want good service and for you to stand behind your company if something does go wrong.

Make sure you honour your big bold guarantee in a very prompt and professional manner. If you don't live up to what you say in your guarantees, you will quickly lose your credibility. Make it right and make it right fast with a smile. Customers are very forgiving if you stand behind what your company does and will become cheerleaders if handled properly once a complaint is made.

Case in point, today on our weekly mastermind call with our franchises, a franchisee was relaying a story about a customer who had called in to say that she thought we had used her vacuum cleaner to suck up some paint and had damaged it. The franchisee knew that it was not his crew who had done this because he was with the crew during the entire job.

He could have said he knew it was not his employees that had done it and left a customer with a bad taste in their mouth or he could have done the right thing. Even though this was a customer that was located a little further out of town, the franchisee turned the situation into a positive one.

He did not get defensive and made a point to quickly go out and check the vacuum and rectify the situation quickly. He went out and looked at the vacuum even though it wound up being something that was not caused by his company. This resulted in creating another cheerleading customer.

The bonus to this story is that the same day he received a referral job from this customer that turned out to be a big job as well. When you think about the lifetime value of a customer, you realize how valuable it is to make sure you honour your guarantees quickly and with a big smile.

He could have left that customer unhappy by saying did not touch her vacuum. Even though this was the truth we didn't risk the chance of losing customer that might talk to others in a negative way about our company. This is a no-brainer when you know that the best thing to do is to make sure your customer is happy.

Chapter 11

Just Because I Gave Janet A Free Spotter Bottle And A Nice Pen She Seems To Always Want To Pay Me Back More

GIVING GETS GIVING AND TAKING MAKES YOU BROKE

It is also called reaping and sowing. It is the law of reciprocity and it is also one of the other principles in the book, "Influence the Psychology of Persuasion," by author Robert B. Cialdini, PHD.

The Principle of Reciprocity states that people repay in kind, whereby the application is "give what you want to receive."

When someone gives a person something, the other person will feel the need to comply. That is why companies give out free samples or gifts. For example, when a salesman gives a pen, a coffee mug, or a shirt to a person, that person will feel obligated to give something back - like a sale.

This is an overpowering rule and reciprocation can be used effectively to gain another's compliance. The rule of reciprocity often produces a yes to a request that, except for existing feelings of indebtedness, would have been refused.

In his book, Cialdini gives an example of how the Krishnas went from a fund raising method to a reciprocity method of giving people the gift of a rose and totally changed their fortunes, producing large-scale economic gains which funded the ownership of temples, businesses, houses, and property in 321 centers in the world.

I remember the first time I was in the San Francisco airport and completely lost. I noticed some people that were in booths that were eyeing me and waving to me to come to them for help. I asked where my departure gate was and they very nicely explained how to get there. As I was about to say thank you and leave, they pulled out a binder of photos of children needing financial help. I was really not in the donation mood but was stricken with the need to help them. I could not bring myself to walk away after they had helped me, even though I felt like I had been set up.

Eventually what happened to the Krishnas was that people made a big effort to avoid them in public places because they knew they were being set up for a hit. Once you have been set up and lead down this path it is next to impossible to dig your way out.

I just heard an interesting story from my Vancouver Island franchise. My contact was telling me that he had just sold a $675.00 carpet-cleaning job and another for $400.00. I asked how the jobs had been acquired and he told me they came from handing out our FREE Room gift certificate.

Years ago, when I would go out into the field to train carpet cleaners, I would unknowingly use the Law of Reciprocity and have much luck. We offered a special on cleaning the Living room and Dining room carpet for $19.95. This would give the customer a chance to see the quality of our service and we would gain a lifetime customer in return.

This method of attracting new customers worked well because it gave customers a chance to use our service with no risk and it was backed up by a bold guarantee. If all they wanted was the $19.95 service, that was fine and they still received service that exceeded their expectations. We gained a customer for life and they gave us a try at a reduced price.

A price leader done properly can be a very powerful marketing tool. If it is not done properly, you may wind up positioning yourself as the cheap service. We were not a $19.95 job company, rather a premium service that was allowing our customer to try our service at an introductory offer.

Funny thing is, if you go into a home with the right mindset you will almost never leave with just a $19.95 job under your belt because the customer will realize that they are working with a home service business they can trust. Once customers trust you they will almost always use additional services.

Back then many of the carpet cleaners would come back to the office with between $80.00 and $300.00 for four calls on a daily basis. They used to say I had horseshoes up my ass because I always came back with $600.00 on a slow day and $800.00 or $900.00 on the good days. This happened to me repeatedly.

The other carpet cleaners wanted to know what smooth sales lines I was using to trick our customers into buying more from me. But it wasn't fast-talking that was getting me the money. It was trust I was establishing with the customer by providing above and beyond service they had never experienced before.

I would throw in extras for free and you could almost feel the exact point in the sales call when the customer knew they finally found a service provider they could trust. Because they had found someone they could trust, and who performed an excellent job it turned into a "while you're here, you might as well do this for me" type of a situation. The amount of "might as wells" kept coming my way all day long.

These customers usually up-sold themselves. I didn't have to be a superstar salesman to earn the highest sales rate of the team. The customer believed my true intention, which was that I was there for them. This was a natural intention that I now realize was the law of reciprocity working for me.

This is a very powerful law and should only be used for good intentions. If used by the wrong people it is very dangerous. Don't use it to trick people. Use it because it is the right way to treat your customers.

I tell my guys to use it because I believe we are the best company to do the work for the customers we deal with. Using the law of reciprocity assures they work with the best company and that a company that provides them adequate work won't win them over. If you can give before you even get started you will push the law into effect, bringing the best results for both you and your customer.

On the same call with my Vancouver Island franchise, the same guy told me about how he had just given out three gift baskets to various customers. I asked if any of the customers started to cry when offered the basket. But I already knew the answer.

One customer who received a basket told Lee the story of how they had moved from the mainland to the island, and had a few bad experiences with other companies in the past. They were blown away by how he had treated them. Our franchisee went on to say that this customer began getting a bit teary-eyed with relief because she had never dealt with a company quite like ours.

She also made it a point to tell us she was going to let everyone she knew what a great company we were and recommend our services. You cannot buy advertising that would be as effective as the cheerleading she was going to do for our company.

This reminds me of another story of how powerful this concept of reciprocity is. This story is from one of our locations that also gave a gift basket to a great customer. I have to point out that all of our customers are great customers.

This customer of ours went into a beauty salon and was raving about our company to all of the women at the salon. She actually had some of our business cards and handed them out. She told them about what a great company she had worked with. One of the ladies spoke up and said she worked with a company that she refused to change from because she was so satisfied. Ironically, that other lady was talking about our company.

Put as many gifts as you can into your customer's hands. We give out company scratch pads, carpet cleaning spotter bottles with lifetime fill ups, and refrigerator magnets. This effort makes us that much more irresistible to our customers and through the law of reciprocity we have increased our chances substantially.

I have seen how powerful this can be when you do the opposite, when thriving businesses fall from grace seemingly faster than freefalling in gravity. You can sometimes see it when a business is taken over by new owners who think they are better fit for the challenge.

A sandwich and soup café with a great following and large lunch clientele was sold to a new owner. The new owner figured out that if he added 10% water to the soup each day, he could raise his profits substantially. What actually happened was that initially he made more profit per bowl of soup but within one year he was not selling very many bowls of soup anymore.

I was also in a chicken restaurant that let you dispense their hot sauce for yourself. You could take a much as you liked. I am sure the owner saw lots of wasted sauce, so he decided to ration it out. You had to ask for a handful of small packets at a time. It becomes obvious when you start getting cheap with your customers.

Your customers will sense when you get cheap with them and the experience goes sour. I have seen it time and time again where the company tries to save money at the customers' expense and they end up losing everything. Eventually customers pick up on the change and will stop coming.

I have seen in my industry where a company will keep their trucks and equipment too long and it ends up costing more money in lost customers than it would have cost to update the equipment. People sense when you are cheap with your equipment and begin to wonder what else you are skimping on.

Don't misunderstand me on this point. I am a great believer in knowing your numbers. The problem is you have to know when being frugal is costing you more than you are saving by sending the wrong message.

You will notice in businesses that do well long-term, that they tend to get the best equipment and supplies that money can buy. As the saying goes, don't be penny-wise and pound-foolish. If you are, you probably won't be in business for very long.

DON'T DRINK THE KOOL-AID IN JONES TOWN

Reciprocity is very powerful and once you include it in your strategy you will be absolutely amazed. We are not talking small potatoes here by any stretch of the imagination. Reciprocity can work for you in both directions. If you steal from people they will steal from you, but whatever you give you will receive ten-fold in return. This has been my experience.

In Cialdini's book, the author gives a compelling example of the power of reciprocity in the account of a woman who saved her life not by giving a gift, but by refusing a gift and the powerful obligations that went along with it. The woman was Diane Louie and she was a resident of Jonestown, Guyana back in November of 1978.

Jim Jones, the infamous cult leader, had called for a mass suicide of all the residents, most of whom drank and died from a vat of poison-laced Kool-Aid. Diane Louie had rejected Jones's command and made her way out of Jonestown and into the jungle. Diane attributes her willingness to do so to her earlier refusal to accept special favours from Jones when she was in need.

Diane had turned down special offers of food when she was ill. She knew that once he gave her those privileges, he'd have her. She did not want to owe him anything. To think that people were that dedicated to their leader that they would commit suicide shows the amazing power reciprocity had over them.

For this book and for your future mental and physical well being, we are using reciprocity for the good of mankind, specifically in marketing our home service businesses. It can be looked at in a few different ways.

If you have the mindset in your businesses that you want the very best for your customers, they will sense that mindset. The prosperity mindset will permeate all areas of your business, just like your customers could sense if you are being cheap. The prosperity mindset or consciousness will attract a very loyal customer to you.

These customers will be as loyal to you as you are to them. These are universal laws and why anybody wants to try to fudge them is beyond me. The penalties for fudging this law have resulted in a graveyard of bankrupt companies. This mindset will be translated into all areas of your business because how we do a thing is how we do everything and that will be transmitted far and broad.

The law can be likened to tithing. This is the practice in certain religions where parishioners give 10% of their income as a tithe to the church. Many authors have written about the benefits of tithing.

Joe Vitale, in his book, "The Greatest Money-Making Secret in History," has written all about the power of tithing and giving. Although it is a small book, do not let its large message escape you.

Another great author who has written on this topic is Catherine Ponder. She has written many books on this topic, but my favourite is "The Dynamic Laws of Prosperity."

HOW MUCH POWER DO YOU NEED?

You want all the power that you can get to help you in your quest to attract and keep customers. You view your company as the best choice for you customer. If you know that the competition is not doing the best for their customers, it is an obligation to make sure that you are the preferred company and that your customers receive the best service.

Utilize the law of reciprocation any way you can. It can be used in any home service business. You might have to brainstorm with business associates but there is always a way to include reciprocation in your marketing strategy. If used correctly, you can double, triple, or even quadruple sales. It takes faith to test this method out to see if it will bring you the returns required to turn a healthy profit.

I have seen restaurants and even grocery stores use this formula with great success. The restaurants gave away a free meal to patrons for trying them out. When you consider the cost of advertising, a response from a free meal can be very effective.

Once the patron tries the restaurant and becomes a repeat customer, the establishment has purchased that customer at bargain. The true secret to any successful business is to keep that customer for life. If that customer does not return, you are in big trouble. Remember that you want customers for life because that is where the big profits are made.

A grocery utilizing this strategy can really win. Many people are loyal shoppers to certain grocery stores because it becomes a habit. When a new grocery store has a promotion for something free that does not require additional purchases, it can really take off like wild fire. The word of mouth to friends and family spreads to people who want to go for the freebie. Usually most customers will buy additional groceries while they are there because it is convenient.

When you consider the cost of giving a few things away for free and the profit made from a long-term grocery customer, it is indeed a very low cost acquisition. You can offer a different free item each day of the week for the first few weeks of business and start your business off with a boom.

The law of reciprocity triggers feelings of trust from your new customers. By giving before receiving, you are generating good will.

THE COMPETITION WON'T EVEN BE ABLE TO FIGURE IT OUT

In my carpet cleaning business we would give away a low price option to attract new customers. We were clear in communicating to the customer that it was only an introductory offer. This gave the customer a chance to try us out and gave us a way to gain a customer for life.

We were careful to not communicate that we were in any way a low price budget home service. This strategy worked really well for us and we attracted a good customer base along with referrals very quickly.

Our competition was overheard saying that we were able to do this because of the government grants that we received. This could not have been further from the truth. The competition was too busy figuring out excuses for their own failure to attract new customers rather than figuring out new ways to build business.

It never ceases to amaze me that there are so many ways to attract and build your customer list and yet the competition is so blinded by their own excuses that they refuse to use these strategies for their benefit. They are so habitual in their thinking that they are blind to new ways of doing things.

The truth of the matter is that not only will they not see your new ways, but they will also defend their old ways with conviction. They will defend their rights to be broke and stupid. Don't you just love it? You don't have to worry about the competition because they spend most of their time putting themselves out of business. They become the Village

Idiot over time and defend their position every step of the way.

I would love to be able to help them all. But I learned years ago that it's better to help people who want help rather than help people who need help. The people who need help but have not asked for it will take your input as criticism and you will alienate yourself. Those who didn't ask for help will drain your good positive energy.

In the carpet cleaning industry, technicians can be the most blinded. They can sometimes be a little like Tim the Tool Man of Home Improvement fame when it comes to equipment. They want those big truck-mounted cleaning plants that are so powerful they could suck your arm out of its socket.

The customer doesn't really care that much about what you use for cleaning, they just want clean carpets. They want friendly, professional service and they want clean carpets. Here lies the difference between the customer and the cleaning technician.

The cleaning technician wants big powerful equipment and the customer wants clean carpets. The technician buys these $40,000.00 truck-mounted cleaning plants that are expensive to maintain and run, and in most cases only clean 500 square feet per hour.

If we use the example of 500 square feet per hour in a commercial carpet cleaning situation here is how the financials break down. At 12 cents per square foot, the truck-mounted plant would make a gross income of $60.00 per hour. Out of this $60.00 per hour the technician would have to pay for gas, labour, equipment depreciation and maintenance. These truck-mounted plants are very expensive to run.

Another option would be to clean this carpet with a $4,000.00 unit that is very inexpensive to operate and can clean 3000 square feet per hour. At 12 cents per square foot you are actually grossing $360.00 per hour and you have very little cost except for labour. There are no gas, equipment depreciation, or big maintenance costs to worry about.

So here is the option, $60.00 per hour and very high operating costs, or $360.00 per hour with very low operating costs. And did I mention the commercial carpet-cleaning customers like the 3000 square feet per hour cleaning machine much better in most cases?

Customers like it better and carpet cleaners make more money, so what is the problem? Believe it or not, it is hard to break the carpet cleaners away from their big equipment obsession.

We had a church that we cleaned three times a year for $800.00 a pop and it took us an average of three hours each visit. That was good money and profitable for our company. The funny part about this job was the person that hired us at the church was a carpet cleaner and he used to do it himself with his big truck-mounted plant. He quit doing it because he made zero money doing it his way.

You would think that he would get one of our machines and start making money again. His mindset had him imprisoned in old ways. This is a common problem in more businesses than you would think. Getting people to change can be as easy as swimming in cold molasses.

Because you are reading this book you have a higher consciousness or awareness and won't let this happen to you. You will be the Village success story that will help anyone that needs help and realize that that is why we are here on this earth.

There is one last point on this subject. A customer does not buy a drill, they buy the hole. They have a problem they want solved and they call you. You are the problem solver. Get out of your own way and remember what the customer wants and it will save you a lot of time and struggle. If they did not have a problem for you to help them with, you would be out of business. This is what your competition can't figure out for the life of them. Their loss is your gain.

Chapter 12

Don't Just Shoot A Machine Gun Into The Air

THERE'S MORE DUCKS IN A DUCK FARM AND YOU WON'T ANNOY THE NEIGHBOURS

Targeting your market is essential to your long-term success. We hear the heroic stories of the salesman selling ice cubes to Eskimos and that is great, but it will make you broke and stupid. Why make your life so tough when it is just not necessary?

VILLAGE IDIOT

You don't want to look like this.

Would it not be easier to sell food to people who are starving? You want to know and choose your market carefully. If your company is a maid service I don't think you would want to advertise in a trailer park mobile home area.

If you are going duck hunting, I don't think you would spend a lot of time in Alaska looking for ducks. If you could, would you rather not go to where all the ducks were? Is that where we get the saying you are a sitting Duck? I digress, but the fact remains that you can become so much more successful and have a happier stress free life if you are more targeted to the customers you are looking for.

In the carpet-cleaning example, I have seen many competitors go completely through an advertising budget by advertising to and targeting the wrong people. It is a waste of money and a waste of time in more ways than one.

There are different segments of customers that get their carpets cleaned. We were a high-end carpet cleaning company that would advertise to mostly professionals and retired people who didn't have the time or know how to do it themselves.

To give you an example of how much difference this can have on your bottom line, I will give you some numbers of what it cost my company if we didn't target the market. If we sent out 10,000 flyers to the south section of a city we operated in, it would cost $1,500.00 in postage and printing. The end of town I am referring to is mostly low-income renters and mobile home dwellers.

In this area I would maybe find twenty carpet cleaning jobs, which meant my cost would have been $75.00 each. If I targeted the mailer to 1000 customers in an area of town that is exactly my target market, I would get sixty orders. The area I am referring to was mostly home to professional couples with high-end homes.

In this example it cost me $150.00 for mailers and cost me $2.50 to acquire a new customer. The big difference in cost was $75.00 versus $2.50 per customer new customer.

This figure does not even take into account the fact that the second mailer, which was sent to our target group, resulted in a better customer and long-term profit. The higher income group is guaranteed to spend more money than the low-income area.

When you mail randomly and don't target your market it is a sure fire way to lose a lot of money fast. You may have the best home service company in the world, but if you don't target your customers you are wasting your time. It is like having a beautiful picture hanging in your closet with the door closed. No one knows it is there because no one can see it.

If you put a fancy restaurant in a mobile home park, chances are it will not do very well. It could be the best restaurant for food, service, and quality but because it is not located in close proximity to its target market, it will lose out.

Think about if you would rather sell purses to women or men. This could change in the future, but for this current time in history it would be a hard sell. If, on the other hand, you had a mailing list of women known to buy a new purse every week through the mail, this could and would be a real gold mine for you. The more you know about what type of customers buy and use your home service, the better off you are.

Knowing how to attract and reach your target customer can be the difference between being wildly successful and stupid and broke. Some business people I have talked to admit that their business was a little slow and often it was a problem of not targeting their customers accurately.

THEY ARE OUT THERE WAITING, AND NOBODY IS CALLING

Have you ever heard your sales people say that it is very competitive out in the field and that everyone is hitting up their customers? In reality, there really aren't that many sales people going after your customers. You are probably asking how that can be.

First of all, when you think about your particular market niche, you will realize that there are not that many people from your niche to even bang on your customer's door. Second, 98% of those other sales people are very unlikely to call on a customer a second, third, or fourth time.

In most markets, your competition is untrained and will give up too easily before the customer is ready to buy. If the old adage that people like to deal with people they know is true, then you had better get to know your customers. This is only achieved through repetition and requires many customer visits.

I think a lot of sales people make the mistake of assuming that their customers are too busy and avoid them. I hear the excuse that the contacts or buyers they have are too busy and sometimes indicate that they will only talk to them through email or request a brochure.

I really have a different take on what's going on here. Yes, maybe the person you want to see is busy but I can almost assure you 100% they are not busy because of other sales people capturing their attention. Many say they are busy because they don't want to waste their time with unprofessional sales people. Many potential customers have had unprepared sales people waste their time in the past and this is the way to screening you out.

Here is the bottom line. If you are selling a home service that will help them, save them money, time, and make their business run more efficiently, it is their job to listen to what you have to say. If you say the right thing in the first 30 seconds and ask the right questions, they will talk to you.

In my commercial carpet cleaning business, I could get appointments to talk to people by being prepared. If I went in and asked if I could clean their carpets, most would say, "Can you send me a brochure so we can have a look?"

This customer response means that they can't be bothered talking to you right now and rather than telling you to get your ugly butt out of there, they keep it polite and lead you on by asking for a brochure. Back when I was still stupid enough to do that, they never called back and I am sure the brochures went straight into the garbage.

On the other hand, I approached them with a clever question like, "If I could show you a way to save time and money with your carpet-cleaning contractor, how would this affect your company?" It is phrased like this for several reasons. First of all, most people will listen to you if you can make their life easier and possibly save them money. Second, I did not ask the question in a way they could say yes or no. If they say no, you sometimes have nowhere to go from there. When you ask how this would affect their company they have to respond by thinking of an answer, which will give you more information to keep the call moving forward.

The first thing you say to your contact must grab their attention just like the National Enquirer grabs our attention in the check out line. You need an "attention-getting" headline.

They are not sitting there waiting for a sales person to come along and keep them company.

You have to provide your customers value and make sure you show them what is in it for them. Once they are hooked in and interested, the rest is a walk in the park.

You have to pull them away from what they are doing and get them interested in what you can do for them. It takes a little planning, but you can always turn your presentation around to immediately grab their attention.

An attention-getting headline is a very powerful strategy that works. Do you want to learn how to market with one? Go get yourself a copy of the National Enquirer. Everybody snickers about the National Enquirer and yet no one will admit to reading the damn thing. The Enquirer sells more newspapers than the New York Times, The Washington Post, The Los Angeles Times, and any other ten major city newspapers of your choosing combined.

Do you want another place to find attention-grabbing headlines of four words or less? Buy Cosmopolitan magazine. Cosmo has been a very popular magazine for decades because they are geniuses at grabbing your attention.

How many times have you watched part of a TV show that you weren't going to watch and then they preview something that is coming up later in the show that captures your interest? Now you are hooked and you can't stop watching because you don't want to miss it. You want to use the same tactic in all of your sales materials and on your sales calls.

WHERE WERE YOU WHEN I NEEDED YOU?

Not only are customers not being called upon, but also many times when they actually need your service, you are nowhere to be found. At the time you make first contact, they may or may not be ready for your service. But you have to be there when they are ready for you and be the first to come to mind when they wonder who can get the job done.

This reminds me of a funny story. In my previous company, we were not perfect and needed to practice. Our company representative had made a sales call to a branch store of a chain of movie video rental shops. The first resistance he got was that all the buying was done though the head office.

Guess what? We phoned the head office and they said the buying was done through each individual store manager. Surprise, Surprise! It was the old "I'll give the salesman a discouraging excuse and then I won't have to waste my time" tactic. The contact probably didn't expect to see us again.

When our representative went back, he offered to do a free demo for the customer to show how well their carpets would come clean. To make a long story short, the customer was so impressed that she was going to recommend our service to all of her local stores so that they should use our company, too. Now that's a done deal, don't you think?

About four months later on a morning telephone conference call with a few of our salesmen, I told the story about how that customer had gone from trying to get rid of us to finally recommending us to all the area stores. I asked how that contract was going, and to my surprise, was told by our representative that we had not been back. We knew better and yet hadn't gone back. You can see now why I say no one is really going after these customers. If we are dropping the ball then the other companies probably don't even know there is a ball game going on.

We of course went back out and made contact with them again. I again inquired the following week how it was going with that customer. Here's the kicker. They had sent someone else to do it because we had not called back. Scary, but true, and then we have to start over again. Think of all the wasted energy this mentality created.

This is the very reason all your customers should be set up on an auto responder. Don't leave chance to the human element when your software auto responder or newsletter fulfillment company can do all the follow-up.

I think it was Woody Allen who said that 80 % of success is in just showing up. With some of the company track records you see out there, you have to agree. You have to stay in contact with your customers so that when they are ready you are their first choice.

I AM SO EXCITED I THINK I AM GOING TO HAVE A HEART ATTACK

The nice thing about all the software and technology available today is that it makes it very easy to stay in touch with your customers. You can stay in touch by either mail or email. Most people are using email and it is a great low cost way to stay in front of your customer.

Make sure you stay in touch with not only your customers who have used your service but also any prospect you have made contact with. These could be prospects you have created an estimate for or people who have just made inquiries.

Get creative on how to attract and keep in contact with your customer list. If, for example, you are a realtor, you could create small ads giving away *7 Secret Strategies for getting the highest price for selling a home*. The customer would only have to give their email address and name and then you can keep in touch by a series of auto-responders.

The cost to do this is virtually free and it is a good way to build your list of qualified leads.

You want to position yourself as the expert in your email correspondence. The more credibility you have with your list, the more they are going to want to deal with you. Remember to always give lots of good information. Your credibility can be built in any number of ways and it is important to be very aware and conscious of this strategy.

When customers are attracted to you because you are the expert, you are that much more valuable to that customer. As mentioned earlier, one of the easiest and most effective ways to become the expert and have instant credibility is to become a published author. It is easier than you can imagine and can really impact your bottom line. Once again, if you see the wisdom in this and would like advice, than contact me at info@servicebusinessriches.com.

Writing resourceful articles is another way to credit yourself as an expert. If you have had an article published in a magazine, a newsletter, or an ezine, make sure you let them know where they can find it. It is always better to show your expertise than to blow your own horn. Most small newsletters and magazines are always looking for good articles, so getting them published can be quite easy.

In your articles you will want to include a hyperlink that will take them directly to your web page. This hyperlink is a very important bit of information and should always be included with any article you write.

It may read like this:

FREE Report Reveals The 3 Secrets That Will Quickly Double, Or Even Quadruple Your Profits In Your Home Service Business, By Bob Burnham, Author of **"How To**

Make A Million Dollars In Your Home Service Business, Guaranteed." http://www.servicebusinessriches.com

You should include this hyperlink on every article you write and submit, and make sure they can only reprint this article if they include it. This is the equivalent of having an army of little virtual salesmen that will keep on selling for you 24 hours a day, 7 days a week.

Make sure that the webpage you send them to is a squeeze page. This is a small one-page website which requires them to provide their name and email address in order to receive the information they are seeking. Some won't, but you will be away ahead of the game just by capturing the ones that opt in. Now you can keep in touch with them and build a relationship with their permission.

Staying in touch with your list of customers will bring you endless riches. You will be surprised at how strong a relationship you can build with your customer just through email. You can personalize your correspondence and let them know a little bit about you in order to strengthen the relationship.

Sharing personal stories with your customers, like telling them that your daughter just graduated from high school, will make you real to them and help them bond with you. Most customers are loyal to the people that they know, so don't miss this opportunity to be you and have fun doing it.

Keep your stories true, but don't miss the opportunity to embellish them, making your story even more interesting. When you keep in contact like this, your customer will buy from you again and again. If they have already purchased from you and you deliver what you say you will, you will find that they are three times more likely to buy from you again. If they have not yet purchased from you, it is likely they eventually will due to the relationship you are building with them through frequent communications.

I bet you can think of some instances in your life when you first met someone that you did not initially like. After a few months or years went by, you found that you became close to that person. Love your customers and they will love you back. Once you get on track with keeping in touch, building relationships, and thinking of ways to attract new customers to your company, miracles will begin to happen. It will be so much fun that you will wonder whether it is legal or not. Just thinking about it gets me so excited I think I am going to have a heart attack.

Chapter 13

Odds Are Near 100% That Leaders Are Readers

YOU CAN FUDGE IT BUT THE ODDS AREN'T GOOD

I was at Dan Kennedy's information marketing summit in Dallas recently and one of the posters that adorned the stage read:

> *"Rich People Have Big Libraries And Poor People Have Big Screen TV's"*

Dan tells the story about how when he goes into someone's office and they have lots of books, and CD's of training materials, he knows he will make a sale. He says he will stay as long as it takes because he knows that they will buy from him.

Dan also says that if he goes into someone's office and they don't have any books or CD's, he will not waste his time and will turn around and leave. Dan is a pretty harsh guy but he sure knows his target market. He knows that people who are always educating themselves are open to anything that will improve their lives. They will be good communicators and always open to new information.

I have noticed that the people who need the information the most will not spend a dime on improving their lives, and the people who need it the least will spend a King's ransom.

It is not uncommon in my business circle that most business owners will spend $25,000.00, $50,000.00, or even $100,000.00 per year on their education. They will spend it on seminars, books, CD's, coaching, and anything that will improve their knowledge.

These people also have a different way of looking at expenditures. They don't look at all this information as costing them anything but rather they look at it as something that makes them more money and that gives them a better quality of life.

Other people look at it as an expense and usually will not spend a cent on self-improvement information. They are too busy whining and complaining that the economy is bad, that taxes are too high, or any other victim story that they can come up with. They tend to look at any information for sale as a rip off and that is why they stay stupid and broke and eventually become Village Idiots.

I would have to say that more than 99% of the time I meet or read about someone who is very successful, I usually find that they are voracious readers. I have heard many others say that most of the people they know who are leaders or who are successful do the same thing. Readers are Leaders. Almost all successful people are avid readers.

I only know of a few successful people who are not big readers. One said he would read but didn't like to, but he must have read enough to get him to where he was. The second did not like reading but he may have been listening to CD's.

I would also venture to say that if you have had some success in the past and if you don't keep educating yourself, the chances of you losing that success are pretty high. I have realized that when I have gone through periods of not reading, my success would dwindle. This is something I will never let happen again.

I have also seen time and time again in my own company what happens when our people are not reading and improving upon themselves. I can always tell when individuals are not reading. It becomes quite evident once you know what to look for. They will fall back asleep and into the mass consciousness and not be as open to forward movement. They tend to be not as positive, faithful, and happy, and it is all because they are not exercising their brains. You either grow or die.

If you read only fifteen minutes per day that won't seem like very much! The difference in knowledge in a particular field will not be much if one person reads a fifteen-minute article. The big gains are made when you read fifteen minutes everyday for a year. All of a sudden those fifteen minutes a day have set you far apart from some one who has not put in the time. You now stand out in that field and could even be considered an expert with those fifteen minutes of knowledge per day.

I have also noticed that successful people will always refer to a book or something they have read and recommend that it can be a helpful resource. These readers will comment that they have read particular books nine or ten times. Not only are they readers but this is also evidence of them being great learners of information.

If you are about to write yourself off at this point because you are not a reader I need to point out the fact if you are not a reader you would not be reading these very words right now. You may not read as much as you should but you have not tied reading to how important it is to your success. You can literally accomplish anything through the information written in books and it will make life a breeze.

IF YOU LIKE MUSIC, YOU LIKE TO LISTEN

You can always use the best alternative to reading to forward your business and that is to start listening to all the different books available on tapes and CD's. This includes marketing and self-help information options. If you like to listen to music, you can easily listen to CD's and tapes.

Get into the habit of listening to them every time you are in traffic. I actually take the long way home quite often because I want to listen to a CD set that will help me move my business forward. I like to listen to CD sets as many as ten times. It becomes a part of my subconscious mind and then my subconscious mind will carry out what it has been programmed to do.

Most average drivers can have the equivalent of a PHD in education within a couple of years. I call this my university on wheels. When my daughters wanted to listen to Janet Jackson, I would tell them that they would thank me one day.

The information available on tapes and CD's today is amazing. Check out Nightingale-Conant at: http://www.nightingale.com. They offer an enormous amount of self-help material that is designed to help you and your business get to where you want to be. You can also find this material in bookstore chains, too.

You can also find many web sites that have recorded information in available in almost any format you want.

They can usually find information that is tailored to your particular industry.

There are several companies out there that specialize in taking popular books and summarizing them into seven or eight pages of information. This is popular with people who especially don't have the time to read a two or three-hundred page book.

IF YOU DON'T HAVE PROBLEMS, YOU DON'T HAVE A BUSINESS

Why am I so adamant about reading and its importance when this is a book to help you market your home service business? Its because the more well read you are, the more you will raise your conscious level of thinking, and the more all this marketing information will make sense to you.

I see so many business people that put off being happy or successful until they get a particular problem out of the way. Your success is in accordance with how well you can respond to and handle problems.

Hungry? There are grocery stores where you can get food easily. Need to get somewhere? There are companies that make cars to help you get to where you want to go. Not feeling well? There are doctors that can help. Life has problems but there are always answers available.

When you constantly work on educating yourself you begin to realize that your problems aren't problems at all, but rather opportunities. I really have to laugh when I see people so focused on getting their problems resolved because the only people with no problems are dead people. After you have figured out and found opportunity in one problem, the universe knows you are now ready for a more difficult problem. Get used to it and enjoy the process because you will never encounter anything that you can't handle.

The bigger the problem your customer has and the better you are at helping him solve that problem, the more money you make. Look for problems and start making some big money rather than avoid problems and go broke. There is no better reason to give someone money then to have a problem solved.

I hereby challenge you to give me an instance where you pay or give away money for any other reason except for when there is a problem that has to be solved. Once you truly understand this principle you will think that people who want to get rid of all their problems are weird.

Remember this important principle: You are in the problem solving business.

As Zig Ziglar said:

'If you help enough people get what they want, you will get what you want."

In other words, people don't have what they want yet, which means they have a problem, and if you help them to solve the problem, you will get more of what you want. It is a great system, but most people are just not conscious of it. Identify their pain and help them. You will be paid handsomely. A lot of business people are trying to sell services and products to people who don't need them. That has to be pretty painful and a hard way of life. Think about what problems they may have and figure out how to show them resolutions.

YOU ARE BIGGER THAN YOUR PROBLEMS

The more you read the more you realize that you are bigger than your problems. You merely want to educate yourself and increase your level of awareness because you are bigger than your problems and they will fall away. How many people say they would love to be rich because they would not have any problems?

I'm sorry, but it doesn't work that way. When you are rich, you have different problems.

Donald Trump would not be worried about paying rent on a one-bedroom apartment at the end of the month because he lives in a multimillion-dollar condo that he has built. A single divorced mother on the other hand might view this as a problem. What is a big problem to the woman is a non-issue to the Donald.

As an example, let's look at the issue of buying a new car on a scale of one to ten. A one would represent no problem at all and a ten would represent a real problem because of a lack of money. The car is a mid-size domestic sedan with a price tag of $18,000.00. For a middle class North American family, this might be considered a five on the scale because it would be difficult for them to afford it. The single divorced mother would consider this a ten because she wouldn't be able to come up with the money. For Donald Trump who would consider this a one, it is not an issue, and in fact he decides to purchase a new Mercedes instead.

The point here is to raise your knowledge, awareness, and consciousness above your problems. Poor people usually accept the fact they have no money and can't afford the new car, blaming everyone else for their situation. Middle class people have the money through employment, but are not usually aware that with a little knowledge and awareness they could greatly improve their lives. Rich people know that anything is possible and seek out the information required to get whatever it is that they need in life.

In Robert Koyasaki's book, "Rich Dad, Poor Dad," he talks about his one dad who always said that they couldn't afford things. His other dad who was rich, asked what needed to be done to afford things. Here are two different mindsets at work, saying everything about how each father lived his life.

The poor dad had nothing and did nothing because he couldn't afford anything. The rich dad had a wealthy, prosperous, and successful life because he always knew that he could find the information he needed to get what he wanted. He had an "I'll do what it takes to accomplish my goals" attitude. We all have that same opportunity, but unfortunately some of us are asleep to this fact and stay within our self-imposed prisons.

Changing your mindset and perspective in marketing will grow or kill you. In my personal business story, I was dead in my thinking for too many years. It was only after I changed one little thought that my whole world started to open up again. Here is my story about changing my mindset.

As the founder and president of Success Carpet Cleaning, I had 600 full and part-time employees and was earning over 6 million dollars in annual revenue by the time I was thirty. I sold most of the company in the mid 80's and ran a smaller fire, flood restoration, and carpet cleaning operation for many years after that.

When I sold my company I was making a lot of money and owned three luxury cars, a cabin cruiser, a beautiful house, took fantastic vacations, and ate at whatever restaurants I wanted to. It was indeed the good life.

Around the time I was selling my business, I met my wife, and in the last nineteen years of marriage we had three daughters, Shay 17, Lex 7, and Sky, who was born this last Christmas Eve.

Even though I had made millions in the past, as time went on, I started to realize that I had an expensive lifestyle. Expensive lifestyles require big incomes and the money I had made wasn't going to last forever. No problem, I thought. I just had to build up another big business again.

The carpet cleaning business had evolved and all the systems and marketing that had worked in the past weren't working as well any more. It seemed like no matter what I did it just wasn't working. I tried everything. The harder I tried the more frustrated I became. My expensive lifestyle continued. This was the only lifestyle my family knew and they weren't interested in cutting back.

I felt like I was on a treadmill, and the faster I ran the faster the speed was turned up. I hadn't really noticed, but for several years I had been saying to myself, *"no matter what I do it just doesn't work."* Then one day, out of nowhere, a blinding flash of the obvious came to me. My mantra had been,

"No matter what I do it doesn't work."

Having a mantra that says nothing works is not conducive to being a successful businessman.

When I was finally tired of being sick and tired and the noose was closing ever so tightly around my neck, a new thought came to me that has truly changed my life forever. I'm sure some of you have lived through this or may even still be living this nightmare right now. I don't wish this on anyone.

What was the new thought that changed my life?

It is so simple and yet so profound that I think we should all be hardwired to think this way, but we are not. Rather than saying ***"no matter what I try it doesn't work,"*** I said to myself,

"What do I have to do to make this work?"

It was almost like a prayer to my higher power. What this new question did was make me truly rich so that I never had to worry about money ever again. The question, ***"what do I have to do to make this work?,"*** became the Holy Grail that catapulted me to the action I needed to take to build a truly successful home service business once again. Halleluiah.

Once I asked myself, ***"what do I have to do to make this work?,"*** it started me on the greatest, most fulfilling journey of my life, and I want anyone who wants to get ahead to join me on this quest. You see, rather than saying, ***"no matter what I do nothing works,"*** and getting those results, I was now asking the question,

"What do I have to do to make it work?"

For me, this was the simple system for creating consistent wealth in any home service business . . .

This question brought me answers or the Holy Grail that truly changed my life. I started reading all sorts of self-help books, going to seminars, and taking courses. I literally read over a thousand books on making my business work. Many weeks I would read over five books per week and I still do this today. I spent tens of thousands of dollars on training. I read the true masters' writings and also some very specialized niche marketing books.

I found trends and wisdom that have been handed down through the ages. Time tested ways, new ways, and never before used until now ways of doing business. Wow! It was a whole new world. I took some of this new information I learned and applied it. And it worked.

Then I tried more and more things, and before I knew it, I was on my way off of the treadmill of doom. These are systems and methods that work to produce incredible results. The first time I had found my great success, I was riding the crest of a wave. This time I discovered what it truly takes to build lasting results and a life my family and I can depend on.

I Truly Never Have To Worry About Money Again. And You, To, Can Have That Same Peaceful Feeling.

What I have learned through years of reading is that thoughts are things and we are what we think about most of the time. You are the sum total of your thoughts. We don't see the world as it is; we see the world as we are. I also learned that our thoughts are habits. We think over 60,000 thoughts per day and most of them are repetitious.

The world is a giant mirror reflection of your thoughts. Do you like what you see? Do you surround yourself with what you want? Are you living the life of your dreams? Are you living in your dream house? What about your car! Is it the car you have always wanted?

The bottom line here, folks, is that I had a problem that almost all businesses encounter. The problem would have ended my business career if I had let it. But by becoming bigger than my problem, and finding out what it takes in marketing to make my business thrive and prosper, I will never have that problem again. I have risen above and beyond those days and have stayed here so that it is now a one on the problem scale and a non-issue for me.

Chapter 14

Holy Cow! Oprah Has One

I AM TOO LAZY TO BLOW MY OWN HORN, AND BESIDES IT DOESN'T WORK

Another strong tool you are going to want to put into your marketing toolbox is "Social Proof", which is another principle in the Robert Cialdini book. The principle of Social Proof states that:

People have a tendency to take an action if there is evidence that many others are doing it. For example, more people prefer Brand A than the other leading brand. Social Proof can be a strong motivator to stay with the herd.

Cialdini gives the example of canned laughter and how nobody really likes it. It is used in television because it works. We have a tendency to see an action as more appropriate when others are doing it even if it is canned. Most of us feel that when a lot of people are doing something it is the right thing to do.

It really is a form of peer pressure and its effectiveness has been documented. You can have a group of people coached to give the wrong response to a question asked by an interviewer and the one person left out of the coaching will have a real hard time not following the crowd by providing a different answer.

Advertisers love to tell us that their service is the "fastest growing" or "largest selling" because they don't have to convince us that the service is good. They only need to say that many others share the opinion, which is proof enough for most.

Another good example Cialdini uses is how producers of charity telethons devote inordinate amounts of time to the incessant listing of viewer names that have already pledged contributions. The message being communicated to the holdouts is clear. "Look at all the people who have decided to give. It must be the correct thing to do."

Why do you think celebrity endorsements are so important for a product success? If Michael Jordan is wearing sneakers, it is an assurance that it is good for us to wear them too. It only takes Oprah to mention a book she liked and it will become a best seller. We trust Oprah's judgement and if it is good enough for her, it is good enough for us.

Cialdini also brings up a very good point about our freethinking youth. We frequently think of teenagers as rebellious and independent. It is important to recognize that typically, this is true only with respect to their parents. Among their peers, they conform to what social proof tells them is proper.

The social proof example that always comes to mind occurred when I was younger and some of my less studious friends found themselves roped into pyramid schemes. I know now that I was wasting my time trying to talk them out of their financial follies. They would always say that the local celebrity millionaires of the time, like their local banker or lawyer was involved, so it must be legal.

These schemes were always going to make them immensely wealthy but it's funny that I never really heard about the losses they incurred after it was all said and done. And what about all the credible people they used as their reason for being so stupid? Where were those celebrities and lawyers now? They always turned out to be another one of those ventures that you eventually never heard another word about. I was too nice to ask what ever happened because they would have only tried to justify their behaviour.

In our company, we used brag books as of way of letting our customers know that we were a good company. I am too lazy to blow my own horn and besides it doesn't work. It is one thousand times more powerful when a satisfied customer puts in a good word for you.

Putting together a good brag book is easy to do and it is an extremely powerful tool. Any companies I have dealt with have found that testimonials are the best way to attract new customers and close business. You should always be collecting customer testimonials for your brag book because it is a sure way to give your customers the social proof they need to make the decision to hire you.

Regardless of what you think about testimonials, they actually work. I am sorry to say that at one time I had a negative opinion of testimonials and for many years I missed out on some of the best business and customers by not using them to my advantage.

You will want to collect customer testimonials and should always have a system in place so you can collect them on a continuous basis. You will be surprised and delighted when you see how fast you can build a huge arsenal of customer testimonials and satisfaction forms.

One of my franchises once had a situation where an adjuster had not approved sending us out to a flooded home until a few days after the flood had happened. The insured's home was starting to smell and the Insurance agent had called and was upset that we had not started the job yet. Needless to say, the claim started off in a bad way. We saw this as an opportunity for our company, and not as a problem.

We finally received approval to start the job, went in and worked our service magic. At the end of the job the customer had turned into a raving cheerleader. My franchisee said he was even a little embarrassed because the customer said she went to work and told her coworkers they should flood their homes so they could use our company too.

You should have a customer fill out a Customer Satisfaction and Completion form at the end of a job, during your customer satisfaction walk through. It is the best time for them to fill one out and you will get the best response when your work is fresh in their minds.

This Customer Satisfaction and Completion form was given to both the Insurance adjuster and Insurance agent, and believe me, this is what they like to see. It makes their job so much easier and you will continue to gain a ton of work from them when you operate like this. The form speaks for itself and is much more effective then you blowing your own horn and telling them that you did a great job for your customer.

Include testimonials in all of your advertising. At the end of this section is an illustration of the cover of our company brag book. I recommend that in a brag book like this you include as many customer satisfaction and testimonial letters as possible. Have three binders if you can because the more you have the better chance you have of sending a positive message about your company.

In addition to customer satisfaction forms and testimonials, you should also have before and after pictures of your work if this is applicable to your business. Even better would be to have a picture showing a side-by-side comparison. Always carry a copy of your business license, insurance, Worker's Comp certificate, BBB membership, along with any diplomas and certificates of training or education that you have. You are the expert and that is why they have you in their home.

If others are using your home service business and like you, this is the kind of social proof that your new customer should consider when evaluating services. Your brag book will begin to build itself with hundreds or thousands of customer testimonials.

I want you to take a minute and envision that this is something you can use in your company. Sometime during your sales presentation you offer your brag books to your customer and say, "Mrs. Customer, here are three books full of testimonials about what our customers think about us. You may even see someone you know." Even the subtle little phrase that you will probably see someone you know gives him or her more confidence to hire your company.

PEOPLE LIKE TO DEAL WITH SUCCESSFUL PEOPLE

The more successful you look in your brag book the better the chances of gaining the customers you want. If you can, use testimonials from VIP'S. Whether it is the town Mayor, Chief of Police, business leader, or anyone important in your community. Put their testimonials in the beginning of your book and let your customers see them first. Building a proper brag book and utilizing it well can double and even triple your closing rate. It will also help you close the customers that are willing to pay a higher price for your service. You have to stand out from your competition, or as author Seth Godin says, you have to be the Purple Cow.

Pictures

Always have your digital camera with you so you can take a picture of happy customers to put in your brag book. Take a picture of your customer standing in or in front of the area of service. It is even better if you are in the picture shaking hands with or hugging your customer. Can you feel the excitement starting to build? The important thing is to have fun with this whole concept and get everyone involved in it.

For a FREE Brag book template, visit www.servicebusinessriches.com/customer-testimonial-template.

Testimonials are very powerful and never underestimate what they can do for your company. Like anything else in life, with an action (showing your customers testimonials) there is reaction (a sale).

YOU HAVE TO APPLY ACTION! Have complete faith because this works. If you want more customers and higher profits then this is an important silver bullet. Use it every time and you will see very quickly that you are attracting more and more customers. See a sample cover of a brag book we use on next page.

BURNMAC SERVICES
"To Exceed Customer Expectations"

We Love Our Customers And It Shows
Customer Testimonials And Cheerleaders

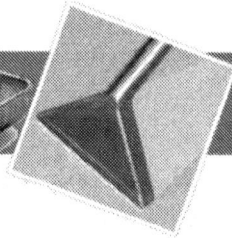

Bob Burnham

1234 Anywhere St. Van. BC. Phone: 123.555.1212

Braggart

No one likes a braggart because they can be boring. No one will want to listen to you brag about your company. It is the third party approach that makes this concept so effective. If I told you my company was great and that we were the best, you would wonder second guess me. But if someone else told you the same information, you would pay attention.

Don't make your customers work too hard to get the information they need. For example, I have seen painters give a list of names and phone numbers to a prospect and expect them to call them all. That is asking them to do work.

You also find that painters will supply only a list of satisfied customers. You should anticipate what questions your prospect may want to ask. If they have to ask you for referrals it is already too late because you have dropped the ball. You can still dig yourself out of the hole, but why dig one in the first place?

There is a good chance your prospect knows nothing about your company. When you present your customer brag book of testimonials, you are eliminating any concerns they may have had before they even come up.

The more confident and prepared that you are on a sales call, the more likely your prospect will choose to work with you. This is especially true if a prospect has had a bad experience with another company.

Any testimonials that are given by people your prospect may know can be very powerful. If you are the home service provider for a local celebrity or well known company, make sure that you get a testimonial from them. People like to deal with successful companies, so don't be shy to have someone well known brag for you.

MAN, EVERYONE CAN'T BE WRONG

I see so many small companies that are making a marginal living and are not using the tools we are talking about. Testimonials, Iron Clad guarantees, and good ad copy can be the difference between being broke and stupid and being this year's business success story.

I have seen many small businesses with mediocre websites. They have websites that look great but that are not functional. The main page does not have a headline that will make you want to read the rest of the page. They have not focused on what is important for the person visiting the site. Not only have they failed to get the visitor to read further, but they have also made a big mistake by not having any sort of tool to capture their prospects contact information so they can follow up.

I see these mistakes being made all the time. It is rare to find someone who is taking the proper steps to market their service in a way that will attract sales. Most are making a minimal effort.

Once you learn all the secrets, strategies, and systems that will help to build your business, you will start to notice all of the people who aren't using these tools and begin to have great respect for the people who are using them. You will recognize the ones who have a few good strategies going and see how they could easily improve on their businesses with just a little of the knowledge that you now have.

Keep your eyes open and act like a talent scout, always on the lookout for new ways to use and expand upon this information. Each little idea and strategy will add dollars to your bottom line.

LITTLE SILVER BULLETS

Don't overwhelm yourself with all of the things that you think you have to change right away. You want to implement and test each marketing strategy, one at a time. Each small change should bring an improvement to the health of your business.

Some changes will bring very small increases in gross income, but when many are used together, they can add up to some very big numbers. Still others will double, triple, or even quadruple your gross income all by themselves. Each time you make a silver bullet change to your marketing strategy and see better results, it may be the change that will keep paying dividends for a long time to come.

This will in turn give you motivation to make more of these marketing changes.

In a regular employment situation you receive a dollar amount for each hour worked. Working hours for money is a very poor path to wealth. Instead, when you make a change to your business plan that brings in residual income, it will have nothing to do with how many hours your work.

If you create an additional way to attract leads, this will be like money in the bank for you. Lets say you are a mortgage broker and you run a small ad in the loans section of the classifieds. The ad prompts readers to call an 800 number or to visit a website to receive "6 FREE Secrets to Getting the Best Mortgage Rate the Banks Don't Want You to Know."

Your leads will be pre-qualified through an automated system before they come into direct contact with you. Once they are in your sales pipeline you can keep in contact with them until they decide to become a customer.

There really are so many amazing low cost silver bullet ways to attract customers to your sales pipeline. Brainstorm with a group of entrepreneurs to come up with more ways to attract customers and soon your contact list will become an asset that puts money into your bank account each and every month.

Chapter 15

And Now Here She Is, Barbara Walters

HERE IS ONE OF THE MOST POWERFUL TOOLS IN THE UNIVERSE, AND IF .01% USE IT CONSISTENTLY, I'LL BUY A PIG FARM

Love your customers! If you want to know how important this statement is you only have to look at the success that Barbara Walters has had. It is a simple, powerful formula.

Barbara Walters is probably one of the most renowned interviewers of our time. She gets interviews with Hollywood stars, politicians, and famous people that no one else can get. Not only does she get great interviews, but also she is able to ask tough questions without offending anyone. She is the best at what she does and there is a little secret behind her success that hardly anyone knows about or understands what great importance it has lent to her legendary career.

On the Good Vibe Radio Station dial, this vibrates at the highest frequency and is the reason she attracts the best people for her interviews. I only found out about it because I am always looking for this type of information. Many of us have this strategy naturally but many don't have it at all. This is where I think Barbara Walters stands out above most.

My wife Marilyn was listening to an interviewer who asked Barbara Walters how she was able to line up such great people to interview and how she has been able to ask such personal questions. Barbara's answer was that while she is interviewing someone, she is repeating to herself, "I Love You," over and over.

That is so powerful and it is just the right way to be in life. Everyone wants to give her an interview and answer her questions. She loves us and we trust her. You can sense her great energy through the TV. This way of relating to her guests has put her at the top of a very competitive industry and I know she will always be there for the rest of her career.

I would be amiss if I did not mention two other successful interviewers that use this universal principal of love to excel in their professions. Larry King loves what he does and also loves his guests and it shows. You will notice he makes no judgments about anyone he interviews and they all feel safe and respond to him positively.

Another on the list is the Billion-dollar person who has come from a tough childhood only to let go of any resentment and rise to the highest pinnacle of success. She has helped more people than almost anyone else on the face of this planet. She also does not judge and emanates more love than a thousand newlyweds. I am talking about Oprah Winfrey.

I read in her boyfriend Stedman Graham's newest book, **"Who Are You? A Success Process for Building Your Life's Foundation."** In it he says that it does not matter if she is talking to the president of the United States or to a welfare mother, they are all treated equally with love and respect. She brings out the best in everyone she meets.

You will notice on her show that she will award and celebrate the successful as well as less fortunate of our society. She does not discriminate even though she was discriminated against during her journey in life.

Following is a great exercise to help you with this strategy. Anytime you are selling a customer your home service, run a mental tape through the back of your mind with these thoughts. Remember, these are your own private thoughts, but they will broadcast an energy that will make the outcome a success for both of you. Choose one of the following affirmations below you feel comfortable with and repeat it several times. If you don't find one below, make up one of your own as long as it has elicits good energy and let the magic begin.

1. I Love You
2. I am so grateful to be working with such a nice customer as Mrs. _____
3. It is great to work with such nice customers as Mr._____
4. I am so fortunate to have Mrs. _____ as a customer. She is great.
5. Bless Mrs. _____. She is so nice.
6. Bless Mr. _____ . He is just the best customer to have.

How powerful is this exercise? Well let me tell you a couple of things first. Once you become truly connected to the Universe through your high energy and kind and grateful thoughts, you will find that the synchronicities will be happening fast and furious on a daily basis. Of course, they have always been happening to you but now you will be aware of them and their constant presence.

Let me give you an example of what I mean. Very recently, one of my franchises was offering a few customer service opportunities. This particular person had only been a franchisee for three months and was only beginning to understand the power of good thoughts.

He was beginning to struggle and was just barely able to complete all of the work that was piling up from attracting new customers through referrals. This is an easy trap to fall into because when you are busy you tend to forget how you got there.

This franchisee had run into opportunities including a customer telling him to finish the job that day or to not bother coming back. Another customer said that she thought a larger amount of work that he hadn't committed to doing was included in the price he quoted her. On top of that, there were a few touch ups that had to be done on completed jobs. It was not a happy time for this franchisee.

I asked him what was happening and he said he really didn't know, but was quick to say the customers he had recently been working with had been a little grumpy. He even gave evidence by saying that the customer who was demanding that their job be completed immediately was the type of guy that would yell at his wife. Apparently he had heard them yelling on a few occasions.

I told him the story of what Barbara Walters does during her interviews and had him refocus and do the above exercises. He had been initially trained this way but he hadn't made it a habit yet.

I went over this information again with him that night. He called my partner Jeff the next day to say he could not believe what was happening with the customers out in the field. He had tried again the methods we had taught him and blessed the customers in the back of his mind while he talked to them.

The customer that had told him to not come back if he didn't finish the job that day was so pleased with his work the out of the blue he gave him a thousand dollar advance on payment. The job was still not finished and yet this man was ecstatic with our service.

The woman that was claiming that extra work should be included in the price became a cheerleading customer. Here is a powerful example of how high energy, and kind and grateful thoughts work to your advantage.

The franchisee was totally blown away by the way the customers were suddenly responding to him. Will he continue to bless his customers? He will as long as he remembers or until it becomes an automatic thought. If he forgets again, he always has us to remind him and keep him on track.

This marketing magic idea is used consciously and unconsciously by some of the most successful people in the world. You will hear over and over again and from very rich people that they find almost 100% of the time that most of the successful people they meet turn out to be some of the nicest people they have ever met. I have also heard people who are struggling in life say that they find some successful business people to be !#%@&.

It doesn't take a lot of brains to figure out which group of people is going to be the most successful.

"Love your customers and the world will be your oyster."

—Bob Burnham

I MEAN, WHY ARE WE EVEN IN BUSINESS?

Entrepreneurs are in business to help customers solve problems and make money. The better you are at solving their problem, the more money you are going to make. People like to deal and work with people who like them, so make sure you are putting out good customer thoughts at all times.

Don't be selective with the ones you like. Love them all and find the best in each and every one. This does not mean you have to approve of everything they do or that you should work for them for free. What it does mean is love your customers and they will love you back and your business will be a booming success.

Have you ever tried picking a fight with someone who just thinks the world of you and loves you dearly? It can't be done, can it? It is almost impossible to not like someone who likes you, so make sure you always love your customers and you will see a marked increase in referrals as well as a much lower complaint rate.

There is a psychological shift we all make when we realize we are on this planet to help one another. Once you take your focus off of yourself and start focusing on how you can best help others, your conscious level rises quickly and dramatically. The more people you like (and everyone has something to like), the better your business will do.

Run fast and don't look back if you find you are standing in a group of business people at your local Chamber of Commerce and they are all whining and complaining about their customers. The Chamber and many other business groups are the best resources and I encourage you to join as many as time will allow, but make sure you don't get stuck in the whiny baby groups. Love them, but don't participate in their whining and negativity.

The whiners will infect you faster than the flu virus so make a quick exit and soar with the ones who obviously love their customers. You will always find that the group that loves their customers and speaks highly of them will always be the most successful group by far. It is not a coincidence that this group does well. This is the right way to operate in business and in life. Make it a life strategy and it will make you wealthy, healthy, and successful.

IF IT'S THE SAME SALES PITCH, WHY IS THERE SUCH A DIFFERENT RESULT?

I have seen this phenomenon time and time again. We train two service or sales reps to say the exact same thing to the prospects, and one will come back with an arm full of orders and new customers, and the other will come back with excuses.

How can this be when they are both saying the same thing to their prospects? What you say to your prospects is only about 10% of what you are communicating to them. I see this in my company every so often when we have hired someone who does not have the same intentions as we do.

I have a good example of a franchisee we accepted that I felt was not right for our organization. A new profiling company we used at the time said he would be a good candidate. I had been interviewing a number of people who wanted to buy a franchise location but I had been turning most away. I felt in my gut that the group of people we were interviewing would not be a good fit.

It was decided that I was being a little to specific in my search for perfect candidates, so we hired an outside profile company who sent us this one candidate promising he would be a success in our company. My gut still told me he was the wrong choice.

The profile company said he had what it took and would be a successful franchisee. My thoughts on this chap were that he had a victim mentality and did not like most people.

This is a time when I did not want to be right but unfortunately was. This new fellow had the lowest closing rate on any estimates we had ever had. New people in our company would close about one in three estimates. As they became confident it would increase to as much as three in four estimates.

(Drum roll please.................................!)

Are you ready for this new fellows close rate? He had the amazingly low close rate of one in six customers, and as time went on it got much worse than that. When I talked to him in an attempt to help him close more sales, he was totally convinced that the customers he had were looking for something for nothing. We were all a little confused and surprised that some were actually quite rude to him.

I want to compare this story with another about someone that started with us a little time later that I thought would do extremely well with our company. He absolutely loved people and especially loved his customers. You never heard him say an unkind word about his customers and on our weekly calls he would always make a point to say he thought he had the greatest customers and was very grateful to have them.

This franchisee had record sales and referrals and did very little advertising. He was literally attracting all kinds of really great customers that contacted him through referrals and heard about him from someone they knew. His sales were four times higher and more profitable than the other fellow who whined about all the things that weren't right about his customers.

I find examples like this absolutely fascinating and it really does show us all the power our private thoughts have in bringing us success or failure. These two franchisees use the same material but have totally different mindsets. One thinks good thoughts and loves his customers, while the other thinks his customers are rude, cheap, and confused. So you have the same verbal message to customers with completely opposite results.

You see this phenomenon in many different franchises around the country. One franchise will be successful and the other will be going broke while both using same system. If you are a franchisor it is important that you have systems in place to attract the right candidates.

Your sales presentation is very important, but if you don't love your customers and have the right intentions for them, you will find yourself in serious trouble.

WE INVITE PEOPLE TO DIE OR GROW WITH OUR WORDS

Every word that is said to a customer should help them get what they want. Put another way, each word you use helps your customer grow or die. Wealthy, healthy, and successful companies are focused on helping others with positive actions and conversations.

Following is an example of the difference between being positive and being negative and the different results the two energies can bring.

We once offered an introductory special that included painting three rooms. When a lead called the office about the special, we set up an appointment to visit them with the intention of both introducing ourselves in person and customizing the offer to their location in an effort to build trust.

At some point in the sales presentation the prospect may ask, "Can you include this extra room in your special because it is small?"

No answer:

"No, Mrs. Customer, we cannot include the extra room because of X reason."

As soon as you plant the word "no" in their mind, you are inviting your customer to die. Many will only hear no and get stuck at this pivotal point. Because they have asked you a question and have not heard what they wanted, they may miss out on any further points you want to make and decide not to hire your company. The word "no" is a word that stops growth and does not help either the customer or the company.

Yes answer:

"Yes, Mrs. Customer, we could include the extra room and because it is small, I will only charge you a very small extra charge of X amount."

Your customer wants to hear "yes" and you should keep their mind open by using positive words that invite growth and carry you forward. I find that the majority of people really want to be fair with you but you really have to stay on their side.

Another good example is the following:

A customer comes up to you during a home show and says in an innocent but slightly confrontational way, "I saw your ad in the paper! Are you going to do my three huge rooms under your special?"

No answer:

"No, we can't do that for you. It only includes three average size rooms and we would have to charge extra."

Once again you have closed off communication and put them in the No zone. Anything you say after that will not be heard. They may even become more confrontational because they do not get what they want. You have put an immediate end to the conversation.

Yes answer:

"Yes, we would love to have you as our customer and would be happy to come out and show you what we can do for you. We are always looking for great long-term customers like you."

You have now invited the customer to grow with you and have broadcasted positive energy and good intentions. You will draw from them positive energy and dispel any negative energy.

As a wealthy, healthy, and successful company, you always want to generate positive energy, have the best intentions and love all of your customers. Do that and you will grow your company beyond your wildest dreams.

Chapter 16

They're Just Not Making Land Anymore

BUT WE STILL HAVE SOME SWAMP LAND AVAILABLE

The principle of scarcity is a very powerful motivator to get your customer to buy. People want more of what they think is scarce. Study after study shows that items and opportunities are seen to be more valuable as they become less available. That's a tremendously useful piece of information for the business owner, salesman, or manager.

I laugh when I think about how this principle has convinced me to buy. Since I have learned this powerful method of persuasion I can think back to the times it has worked on me. Even now that I understand the principle, I sometimes don't realize this still happens to me. I could very well be that the principle is being applied or that there is an actual shortage of that product.

This method is probably recognized by most when it is in the form of a limited time offer. For instance, "If you don't buy this car today it will go back up to the regular price and you will lose out." Many recognize this method as a ploy to sign on the dotted line today, yet many of us have no idea this is being done to us.

In his book, "Influence," Robert Cialdini refers to one of his students that owned a meat business and the scarcity experiment they conducted. The owner of the meat business had his salesman split his customers up into three groups. The first group was treated in the usual manner of sales and order taking. The second group of customers was told there was a shortage in inventory coming up, and the third group was told that they were privy information on an upcoming shortage of inventory.

The results showed that the difference in sales between the three groups was quite dramatic. The first group ordered their regular order. The second group ordered twice as much. The third group had an even more dramatic reaction. Because the third group was told that they had inside information on an inventory shortage, they ordered six times their regular order!

My favourite scarcity strategy is the story of a grocery store that put a product on display with a limit of six per customer. Now I know that I have encountered this before and I have purchased six of something when I had the intention of only buying one. Because there is a limit of six per customer we think that we should stock up now, resulting in more money for the grocery store.

I remember years ago when I was looking at buying a new Corvette. I had been hemming and hawing with the salesman about whether I should buy it or not when I looked out the window and noticed that someone else was going to take it for a test drive. Seeing that person about to drive my new car away pushed me to want to get that person out of the car because it was mine.

The exact same thing happened to a friend when he was looking at buying a new BMW. Someone was getting into it for a test drive while he was trying to decide and the next thing he knew, he was buying the car. I did not realize until many years later that we had both been persuaded to buy the cars through the principle of scarcity.

Robert Cialdini's brother sold cars and he used scarcity tactics very successfully. He would list the car for sale in the paper with a great ad that would attract a lot of callers. Rather than schedule appointments at different times, he would make them all at the same time. He would make one potential buyer wait while the other was looking at the car and this made people fear that they would lose out. Needless to say, he sold cars quickly and at a good price with this strategy.

You must always consider incorporating the principle of scarcity into your offers. It must be a legitimate offer and you must come up with a reason for the offer. If the offer extends until a certain date, you must give a reason why. This helps to create the urgency that if customer doesn't respond by a certain date then the price will go up to a certain amount and they will lose out.

There are many ways to build the principle of scarcity into your offers. You just have to be imaginative and then give a good reason. It could be that you are overstocked or that the model year is changing and you are able to save them a substantial amount of money while the quantities last.

I was just talking to a friend and I asked him how the office he was building was coming along? He told me it was coming along quite nicely and that he was ready to install windows. I told him that he had better hurry up because I had just heard that there was a glass shortage.

His reaction was quick and bold. He said, "No way! I had better hurry up." At that point I told him I was testing my scarcity principle on him and not to worry. He was glad to hear it. Give it a try you will be totally impressed with how well this works.

We have had new white van driving through our neighbourhoods making a fortune on the scarcity principle. They would scour parking lots for people they thought would like to buy stereo speakers. They would pull up behind your car as you were getting in or out of it. The passenger would yell to you asking if you would like to buy a new pair of high quality stereo speaker for a big discount. He would go on to say that they had a shipment that they had to liquidate today and that you could save a considerable amount of money.

If you sounded somewhat interested they would invite you to look into the back of the truck where they had several pairs of brand new speakers. They would go on to say that because they had to get rid of them, you would save almost 80% off the price. Rather than having to pay $800.00 you could have them today for $200.00. They sold a lot of speakers and made a lot of money this way.

The truth of the matter was that they had you on the scarcity and greed treadmill. Most customers didn't realize until they got them home, if they ever realized it at all, that they were in fact $100.00 speakers sold for double the price. Most people don't like to tell you they have been ripped off and in most cases will defend their buying decision.

These criminals were eventually stopped but it is a good example of how scarcity can work. It was reported in the paper that these fellows in the white trucks had actually made millions of dollars this way. How many speakers do you think they would have sold had they said they had $100.00 speakers that they wanted to sell for $200.00?

Marketers that are employing this strategy are making enormous amounts of money. They are always positioning themselves to make more sales through good direct response principles.

WILL I REALLY BE THE ONLY ONE?

Many people like the idea of belonging to an exclusive club. It could be a golf club or something they have purchased that adds prestige. Collectors buy valuable coins because they think they have the only one or one of a few in existence. It is through the scarcity of the coin that extra value is created.

You can make your home service scarcer by any number of ways. You could have an expiry date or limit the number of customers that would be able to acquire a certain service. Get creative and be careful not to give everything away. A good example may be that you give away something free to the first 50 people that respond to your offer.

Have the offer provide something of value and keep in mind other things you can sell in addition to the offer. I have seen restaurants that will give away a free half chicken when a customer chooses a baked potato and a salad to go along with it. If you gave away the whole dinner you would not have the opportunity to make any money. Be careful with this strategy and think it through.

I must also caution you that any time you make a limited time offer or a limited quantity offer, you must have a legitimate reason for doing so. If it is not a real sale, your customers will smell a scandal.

Any time you are about to raise your prices on any of your services, make it an event. Let all of your customers know that you are raising your prices on a specific date, and because they are a preferred customer, they can still purchase at the old price until then.

I have seen companies raise their prices and not turn it into an opportunity. Usually they just send a letter saying they are raising their prices and wanted to notify their customers. How negative is that? Take that negative and turn it into a positive by letting people get in on the opportunity because they are part of a preferred customer club. Now that is a positive way to announce an increase in prices.

"We have 25 cookbooks and will give you one FREE if you are one of the first 25 people who book an appointment to have their furnaces serviced this week. Please note that we are only able to offer a cookbook to the first 25 people who book their appointment, so call in right away!"

Watch what other industries are offering and then adapt the ideas to your business. Once you get into the creative flow of doing business this way you will start to come up with endless ideas for limited promotions. You can find more examples in my Home Study course available at www. servicebusinessriches.com.

LET THEM IN, AFTER ALL, THEY ARE YOUR PREFERRED CUSTOMERS

You will always want to make sure your customers know they are part of an exclusive club or membership. As part of this exclusivity, you will want to give them certain privileges that are exclusive to them. You might include a discount or a little something extra, because after all, they are a preferred customer.

This has advantages for both parties. First, it makes them feel special, and second, it is a way to build customer loyalty. You see it with many grocery stores, but rarely is it done by home service businesses.

Preferred customer clubs can be set up many different ways. You can automatically give them privileges by just being a repeat customer, or you may up sell them the privileges if they join a club. It could be an annual fee of X amount but it would include special bonuses that are not available to other customers.

By joining your club they could receive an extra consultation that is worth more then what they paid and could include a guarantee. There is no end to the different ideas you can come up with to make your home service more interesting.

Your customers like it when you are a recognized brand and any way you can do this is a win-win situation. Always make sure you thank them for their referrals with a card or gift.

Chapter 17

Warning!

WARNING! DO NOT READ THIS CHAPTER, AS IT WILL PERMANENTLY CHANGE YOUR LIFE

Warning!!!! Do not read this chapter. Under no circumstances should you read this chapter, because once you know what is in this chapter, it will change your financial life forever. I have warned you so please just go to chapter 18 right now and never look back.

If you are still reading this it is because you are a rebel or you just can't stand not knowing what is in this chapter. I will warn you one last time to please go to chapter 18 and never come back and read the information in this chapter.

Well, if you are still reading this, I want it to be worth your while for being such a big risk-taker with your life and your financial future. I want you to be rewarded because once you know this information you can never unlearn it and go back to the way things once were.

I am going to tell you a secret that will change your life forever. This secret has made everyone that uses it rich. It is a skill so powerful that it will create a huge financial windfall for you. It makes people open their wallets and give you money on a regular basis. The skill I am talking about sells billions of dollars worth of products and services every year all over the world.

Some people get paid as much as $35,000.00 plus commissions in the millions for a single job. But I emphasize that you should not be reading this. And I know that you are reading this right now because I have you hooked and you can't stop reading. You have to know what this powerful secret is.

This secret has worked for authors, business people, publishers, and even individuals just trying to make a little extra money. I have to admit I was a little slow in seeing the value of this secret because of my limited beliefs, but now I just love using this secret because it is like printing money on demand. I now only think in terms of projects where there are big dollars because the secret will work just as easily for a high dollar project as it will for a low dollar project. So why waste time with small dollars?

There are people making hundreds of millions of dollars with this secret. If you knew this secret would make you a million dollars, how much would you pay for it?

This secret has made books into bestsellers and has kept them on the bestseller list. You just don't see this secret used that often because most people aren't aware of how powerful it is. I have seen some pretty young people who are aware enough to use this secret driving around in $200,000.00 sports cars.

One person I know of not only owned several $200,000.00 sports cars, but also spent much of their time traveling the world driving high priced sports cars as a hobby. This fellow knew the power of this secret and used it to fund his expensive hobby.

If you can read and have a conversation, than you can utilize and learn this secret. It has been used on you and has gotten you to pull your wallet out and hand over your hard earned cash on many occasions. If you are still reading this even though you have been forbidden to, then I should probably let to know what the secret is.

COPYWRITING

Why is copywriting so powerful? When you know how to use direct-response copywriting, you can have people buy more of your product or service by just the use of your pen. Killer copy can make sales skyrocket 300% to 400% and much higher. A good sales letter with good copywriting can generate millions of dollars.

If your business is big enough to afford a good copywriter, I recommend you find one, because the returns will be staggering. I must warn you though that the costs for a good copywriter can be a high. Make sure you have a referral for a good copywriter and realize this is where you don't want to be cheap. I can refer a good one to you at info@ servicebusinessriches.com.

If your company is not big enough or in a position to hire a copywriter, then copywriting is one of the most important skills you can learn. Don't let the skill of copywriting intimidate you because if you can hold a conversation, then you can write a direct response sales letter. There are many good copywriting courses on the Internet and all kinds of help and resources available. Have fun with it and please let me know about your success stories. I like to publish success stories to motivate us all to go for it.

What's The KEY SECRET To Increasing Your Response Rates By As Much As 1500% — <u>At No Cost Whatsoever</u>?

In a word, it's your HEADLINE. Your headline can make or break your response and should always be tested. You have to **"Grab Your Customers By The Eyeballs"** and make them want to read your copy.

Most companies fail miserably when it comes to writing headlines. They either don't use one at all or they use their company name. The company name might have a strong emotional response to the owner of the company, but the customer could not give a rat's ass what your company name is.

In the carpet cleaning industry I have see many of my competitors using a picture of their trucks as the headlines. Some have pictures of several trucks, and although I am sure my competitors are proud of all the trucks they own, their customers could not care less. Don't make mistakes like using ineffective headlines that don't grab your customer's attention.

Headlines command attention. Most of us have a tendency to read headlines first, before reading the copy. Headlines stand out visually, thus compelling people to pay attention to them first. Headlines act as titles and lead-ins that are set above and are clearly separated from the rest of the copy. This naturally attracts the eye of the reader.

According to advertising legend David Ogilvy, five times more people read headlines than the body copy of an ad. If the headline fails to stimulate interest, the reader simply moves on. With five times the readership, headlines have a unique opportunity to make any message very successful.

You only have a few seconds to get your message across and to grab your customer's attention, so make sure you have a good attention-getting headline. Start by writing as many rough headline ideas as you can. Your first headline probably won't be your best work. But as you continue writing, you'll find better ways to express your thoughts in a more compelling, provocative, or interesting way. I know copywriters who recommend that you start by writing one hundred headlines.

Separate out your most impressive and unique competitive advantages. Why will your customer want to use your company? Take your unique advantage and turn it into a persuasive sales message.

There are many headline generating products for sale on the internet to help you. Some have hundreds of successful headlines as examples to get you thinking of how to produce a great headline. A great headline can be used for a long time, so it is worth putting the time and effort into making one that works.

Following are a few recommended copywriters that are at the top of their field. They sometimes take on new clients.

Red Hot Copy - Lorrie Morgan Ferrero
http://www.red-hot-copy.com/

Perry Marshall
http://www.perrymarshall.com/copywriting/

Michel Fortin
http://www.successdoctor.com/

You can also find many books and home study courses on the internet that can help you with copywriting. Some good ones are:

Yanik Silver
http://www.instantsalesletters.com/

Instant Headlines
http://www.red-hot-copy.com/instantheadlines.
htm#ORDER2

Lastly, another way of finding a copywriter is through Elance:
http://www.elance.com/cgi-bin/rd/myelance/main/my-elance.pl?source=index

With Elance, you can post your project and have a number of copywriters bid on your job. You can also check their references to make sure the other customers have been happy with their services.

WHAT BOOK WOULD YOU READ?

Once you study copywriting, you will become a more compelling writer and draw in your audience. Below is a fictitious example of a table of contents. A is the standard poor example you see in books, and B is an example of how some people write books that draw you in with a more compelling copywriting style. Which one would make you not want to put the book down until it was finished? A or B?

Chapter 1
    A. In this chapter we discuss how to be happy and have more.
    B. The "How to" Guide of little known but powerful secrets for happiness and money.

Chapter 2
    A. In this chapter we discuss what action to take to grow a business.

    B. Discover the cash exploding secrets hidden in your
       business.

Chapter 3
    A. In this chapter we give you the information for you to
       make your business more money.
    B. The miracle of compounding your money.

Chapter 4
    A. In this chapter we discuss how to be successful.
    B. Give me just 3 hours and I will show you the secrets
       of some of the country's most successful businesses.

Chapter 5
    A. In this chapter we discuss how to work faster.
    C. How to develop a Zen-like power of concentration to
       get twice as much work done in half the time.

Chapter 6
    A. In this chapter we discuss how to be nicer.
    B. How to develop a magnetic personality and discover
       the 5 secret loving traits we are all born with.

I have actually seen some books written with the A style format, if you can believe it. It actually sucks the life right out of you thinking about having to read the information presented this way. The B style format develops an "I can hardly wait" type of response with the reader being anxious to devour this great information.

    I really don't think there are too many people who would not be more compelled to read book B as opposed to book A. If you think about the book that has really captured your mind and you just can't put down, it is the book that is written using sales letter style copy.

One only has to look at the long-term success of a book like "Think & Grow Rich," by Napoleon Hill to see how being a great copywriter can make you a great author as well. Following are a few of Hill's chapter titles and subheadings from that book:

- Why Men Seldom Succeed Before Forty
- The Greatest Of All Mind Stimulants
- The Storehouse Of Personal Magnetism
- What I Would Do If I Had A Million Dollars
- How To Transmute Ideas Into Cash
- The Secret Of Mental Power
- Why You Are "The Master Of Your Fate"
- Miracles Of The Sixth Sense

The whole book is written with tittles and subheadings like these. So many people say this is the book that changed their lives and I never realized until Dan Kennedy pointed out that Napoleon Hill was a part time copywriter in order to support himself while he wrote "Think & Grow Rich."

I know when I read a book late into the night, I can't put it down until I know "Why Men Seldom Succeed Before Forty" or "The Secret Of Mental Power." You have to know the answers to those teasers and that is what keeps you engaged.

GOLD IS MADE IN COPYWRITING

Whether you study copywriting yourself or hire a good copywriter, the payoffs will be enormous. You will find you can use this tool in any area of your business. It is used in newspaper ads, websites, direct mail, email, radio, television, and anywhere you want to capture your market. If you find a sales letter is working in one media, most likely it will work in other media.

An eye-grabbing mind-stimulating headline followed by compelling sales copy will always outdo your competitors who probably aren't using this tool. I could have named this book:

"Operating A Home Service Business"

"The many things you need to know to run a home service business"

Would you have bought this book with a title like this? Maybe, but I doubt it. I know for sure a lot more people will buy this book with the title:

HOW TO MAKE A MILLION DOLLARS IN YOUR HOME SERVICE BUSINESS

Discover The Secrets To A 6 Figure Income From A Front Line Entrepreneur

I am appealing to you in many different ways with this title. First, who doesn't want to make millions? Second, it is a big bold claim with a guarantee. Third, the subtitle appeals to you if you want fast increased results in profits. Fourth, you just don't want to work that hard.

I was scrutinized by a couple of people who asked me if the title is true. After they scrutinized me they realized that I had made millions of dollars with my systems and that they are true and do work. This title and subtitle grabs most people's attention, even if only to buy the book to find out if it is true or hype.

The more copywriting you do, and the more it brings you success, the better your passion will be to keep improving this special talent. The name of the game is Test, Test, Test, and then after that you test again. Testing is such a huge part of direct response and copywriting because very small changes often do bring really big results.

You will learn when you study copywriting that how you structure your sales letters with guarantees and testimonials can make or break your sales. For example, if you have a testimonial just above your headline, it may not be as effective because the headline is now competing with the testimonial.

The easiest way to familiarize yourself with copywriting is to check out all the different sales letters that are on the internet. Check out some of the electronic information products that are selling well on www.clickbank.com. They are listed in order of best selling to worst selling. You will find that the best selling products, in most cases, will have really good sales copy.

Chapter 18

Referrals Are Better

THE ONLY COST OF A REFERRAL IS DOING THE RIGHT THING

All businesses should have a referral collection system in their arsenal in order to grow their customer list. It is reasonable to assume that if the customer you are doing business with right now likes your company, then many of their friends could also be perfect customers, too.

Have a system in place to collect referrals from your customers. There are many ways to do this. Be creative and try a few different ways. In our case, when we are doing the final walk through to make sure the customer is satisfied with our work, we will say something like this:

"Mrs. Customer, it is so great working with such a nice customer like you. You must have friends that are nice like you that would be a good match or referral for our company."

Sometimes the customer will give you a couple of names, but if they don't, you can give them a special customer referral card to give out to their friends with a premium or bonus bucks that will give them an incentive to give the card out.

Some customers will give you five referrals and some won't give you any, but you will consistently build your list. Even if only one in four customers give you a referral, that is a 25% increase in business. If you get four out of four customers, you have just doubled your business. Doubling your sales from your current customers through referrals is an easy process once you begin to focus on it.

When you know how much profit is in each customer you acquire, this gives you incentive to keep acquiring new ones. It really is a no brainer because the customer you are doing business with right now will be inclined to refer you and tell others about what a great company you represent.

Test and practice your referral gathering system in order to make improvements to it and to increase your acquisition rate. The better your company is at "wowing" your customers, the easier it will be to get referrals. It makes your life easier as the business owner because acquiring referrals from your present customers will be a natural by product of just doing the right thing for your customers.

The happier your customers are, the more willing they are to give you referrals. The happier the customer, the happier all your staff will be, too.

You will find that when you aren't getting as many referrals with this system, its either because your staff is not asking as often, or there could be a customer service problem. The amount of referrals you get is a good barometer to test how your business is actually doing.

So many business owners want to know how to increase their revenues and this strategy is the answer. If you can't increase your sales by at least 25% immediately by applying this strategy, you will want to first check that your customers are happy with the service you are providing.

As you tune up and get more imaginative with your referral strategy system, your sales will increase exponentially. Get lots of input from your employees as well as mentors, coaches, and brainstorming partners. Each time you refine the system it will show increased sales results and dollars in your pocket.

We as business owners are always sitting on gold mines, but we must be vigilant miners. Don't overwhelm yourself with trying to implement too many strategies at once. Take one at a time and build on it and refine the process and then move to the next one.

The most important aspect of referrals is most certainly showing appreciation and a thank you is a must. If you don't say thank you and reward your customer, I can guarantee it will be the last referral you will get from them.

Always find out from all new customers that call you where they heard about you so you can send a thank you to the customer that referred them. Gratitude is one of the most powerful energies in the universe and should be practiced at all times with your customers.

Keep the universal flow going by maintaining a grateful attitude and thanking your customers every chance you get. Have a system in place to send thank you cards because as you get busier it is easy to forget and fall behind.

THEY'RE CHEAPER TO GET AND PAY MORE MONEY! IS IT CHRISTMAS?

Referral acquisition costs implemented properly cost you nothing. If you are already in the customer's home or in your business location and in front of the customer, it is not going to cost anything to ask them to get them to give you a few referrals.

In most businesses today, the cost of acquiring a new customer can be high and many companies won't make any money off their new customer until the second time they buy. Acquisition costs include ads, print media, radio, and television, and these can all be substantial. This is why it is so important to take advantage of the opportunity when you are standing in front of your customer for no cost.

The customers that are referred to you buy their friends are much less price resistant and are easier to work with. Referrals already have the trust element built into the equation before you even do business with them. Your acquisition costs are zero in most situations and your profits are higher because of less price resistance.

This is a good example of doing the work once and being paid over and over again for the same work. You put the referral system together and train your people to follow it and now you are paid on a regular basis for the work you did once. There is no reason to not implement this strategy in one form or another.

The only reason you would not want to implement this system is if you love being stupid and broke and you think you have a good chance to win the 'Village Idiot Of The Year' award. In your local business circle there are a lot of people competing for this award already, so don't bother.

I know some of you will be shy and think you are a being too pushy if you use a system like this. If you think you are being pushy by having your customers refer their friends to the best company money can buy, then maybe you should go home a get a job flipping burgers. Go for it because you deserve the best life possible and so does your family. Get out there and play around with it and make it fun.

You can start in a very low-key way and fine-tune it as you get more confident gathering your referrals. If you have done a great job for your customer, they will do a great job for you. This is a universal law. People like helping people who help them, so get out there and exceed your customer's expectations and ask for referrals and the customers will love you.

In addition to testing different approaches for getting referrals from your customers, you can also track your increase in sales. As you see the significant increase in sales this will motivate you to keep refining and increasing its effectiveness.

Always remember that the difference between first and second place in an Olympic event may only be a matter of a 100th of a second but the difference between gold and silver is enormous. Referrals can put you in the business annuals as entrepreneur of the year, so go out and go after the gold.

EVERYTHING WE DO IS A HABIT. WHY NOT HAVE GOOD ONES?

One of the biggest issues I often face as a businessperson is to break old habits. We tend to do the same things day in and day out, but for some reason we expect different results. Is that not the definition of insanity?

I fight this habit-forming paralysis with franchises as well. They go out and do the things they are used to doing and are comfortable with. The problem is when we get into that habit-forming mode of doing the comfortable and not trying the new things, our lives remain the same.

This is why you will want to instill new habits in the people you work with so that these new habits will bring new results. The example I will use here is the habit of asking customers for referrals. You will want to make your own system and presentation, but using the one in my company has paid great dividends.

If our guys get into the habit saying upon payment for the work:

"Mrs. Customer, it is so great working with such a nice customer like you. You must have friends that are nice like you that would be a good match or referral for our company."

You will notice the return energy exerted is very substantial. After your staff is over the procedure of being new, awkward, and uncomfortable, it becomes a profit producing habit that you would never want to break. We all have habits, both good and bad. You want to focus your staff onto the habits that bring in maximum returns and make your company a great place to work.

Trade in the habits that produce lower dollar activities for ones that produce high dollar activities. A low dollar activity for one of my franchises would be painting a wall or cleaning a carpet. You will never get rich doing either of those activities. You can pay someone else anywhere from $10.00 to $25.00 per hour to do it for you.

Acquiring a new customer could result in a $34,000.00 to $52,000.00 lifetime value. Every time you acquire another customer you are supplying hourly work for your staff. A good habit to focus on would be to refine a referral generating strategy that gets you a $34,000.00 to $52,000.00 customer and not a $10.00 to $25.00 per hour job.

It's obvious what choice to make, but I see small businesses wasting their time on low dollar habits all the time. When asked why they are not concentrating on high dollar habits, they will tell you they are just too busy.

They are too busy all right. They are too busy being stupid and broke. You hold the key to your prison cell. Let yourself out and enjoy the unlimited potential of building your business to wealth, health, and success. You are only limited by your own self-limiting beliefs, so replace them with possibility and the habits that will take you and your business to great success.

THE NEXT REFERRAL COULD BE A JACK POT

Do you like fishing? I liked it when I was a kid because I did it with my father. It was exciting because you never new what kind of fish you were going to pull into the boat. After I made my first million, I bought a boat that we took out on the ocean off the west coast of Vancouver. In the ocean, you really never knew what you could bring up from the deep.

You could experience a huge struggle and think you are going to pull in a huge fish and it turns out to be a small 9 pound dogfish that fought like a 50 pound fish. You never know what is going to come into the boat, so you keep right on fishing and expect the prize.

Some days the prize is fun on the boat, but the next week it may be a 45-pound salmon. Now that is fun and it is what keeps the fishermen coming back for more. It only takes scoring one big one for it to be a raging success for the year, but lets face it, the more often you have your line in the water, the better your chances of the next big catch.

Referrals aren't any different than fish. You get some referrals that can absolutely change your life and some that are just another day's work. When you look at all your different marketing strategies as a way of landing the next big one, it will become so much more fun and you will attract all the big fish you can handle.

I know when we start out our new franchises the people involved have different ideas about what to expect from their customers. Depending on what type of economy they have lived in before buying a franchise, they may think that a

$2,000.00 paint job is a big job. As they get more used to the business and start to understand what potential jobs can be like, they will begin to visualize larger and larger jobs.

If you have your systems in place for constantly generating new customers you just never know what you may pull out of the customer ocean. Once you have set in motion these habits of expanding your business through lead generation and referrals, you will find the whole universe will open to you.

All of a sudden you may be handed the right book, or meet the right contact that will move you along the path to success. It is through your intention to expand that you will attract all sorts of great opportunities that you would never have seen before.

People looking in from the outside of your business will think you are lucky and always in the right place at the right time. You know differently because you will have created your own luck. Through systems and habit-forming processes, you increase the odds dramatically in your favour to win big.

I have had many great successes over the years and they almost always come from the most unexpected places. I have had someone start in my employ that was able to raise sales through a different sales lead generator. That tip increased sales by 50% and it was through the act of hiring someone new and being open to new input that made this a reality.

Previously, a good paint job may have been bid at several thousand dollars for a new franchisee, today we have $200,000.00 estimates. The $15,000.00 to $40,000.00 painting jobs are commonplace as we become more aware of what is out there and keep our referral generating systems working for us.

We will attract to us a customer that refers many customers to us because of great service quality and established trust. Sometimes you can go a while with small successes and then have a rash of many great new customers through our referral system. The referral can be a customer that might put an extra $200.00 or $100,000.00 into our pockets.

You just never know when you may land the next really big one. You just have to keep your line in the water and constantly be on top of the fresh bait. I guarantee that if you keep up your referral systems and strategies they will change your life and make you a very wealthy, healthy, and successful entrepreneur.

Every time you ask a customer for a referral you get another chance at winning the jackpot. The nice thing about this lottery is that you increase the odds to your favour. Your results are assured unlike the 1 in 10 million chance of winning money through your local lottery. Get in the game and become a sure winner with lots of big and small prizes and no limit to the amount of times you can play. Good Luck will be with you because you are creating it each step of the way.

Chapter 19

Don't Compare Apples To Apples, Compare Apples To Oranges

FOR 23 CENTS A DAY YOU'RE A GOOD BUY

As a business owner you will often be held up and compared to the competition. Customers have been trained to do this, but we don't have to play by their rules. These rules state that the customer would like to know what your company is going to give him in comparison to the competition.

That rule just plain stinks and you aren't going to play that game anymore. There are a lot of ways to work around this rule. You don't want to be compared to another company with price, benefits, level of service, or any number of unknown variables.

You want complete control of all the variables of the sales process. It is ultimately better that your customer continues to work with your company because you are the best at what you do and this is the reason you spend time reading books like this.

Let's look at an example a person that provides landscaping services to homeowners. Mr. Landscaper knows he has to charge $100.00 per hour to give good value to his customers and to make a profit. A lot of companies tend to go head to head on hourly fees with their competitors, but because you are now out of the rat race, this is what you will do.

You will have calculated that to service this customer it will take 3.5 hours per month. At $100.00 per hour this means the customer will be paying $350.00 per month. If the customer wants to know your hourly rate, let him know you charge by the contract and not by the hour. This way if some months it takes a little more time, you will not be coming to them for more money.

Now you can let them know the details of what you are going to do for them. Your service includes raking, cleaning, seeding, trimming twice per month and power washing twice per year, etc. Once you have told the customer all the great things that are included in the package you have put together for them, you will say it only costs $11.80 cents per day. You could also provide a weekly rate of $82.60. This has the customer more focused on what he will get rather than what he is paying. You don't want your customer making a decision based on the lowest hourly rate they can secure.

You don't ever want your customers comparing apples to apples. Instead, you want them comparing apples to oranges. You also have control of this approach in your print and copywriting sales letters. Break your offer down and show them how your service compares to other factors but not your competitors prices.

SHOULD YOUR CUSTOMER BUY FROM YOU, YOU, OR YOU?

One of the quickest and best ways to put extra cash into your pocket in any home service business is to sell your services in packages. When you sell your services in packages, you quickly separate yourself from the competition.

For example, a customer gets three estimates to paint the interior of their home, and the three estimates are $1,500.00,

$1,400.00, and $1,300.00 consecutively. Sometimes you will find customers who take the high price, some will go for the medium price, and other will take the cheapest price.

If you set up your home service business to show a customer three available packages like in the example below, you have changed the playing field dramatically. Your customer is now deciding between you, you and you, rather than between you and your competitors.

Following are a several good examples of packages we have used in the past:

BURNMAC SERVICES
"To Exceed Customer Expectations"

Platinum Package # 1

Furniture Moving
Furniture will be carefully moved and replaced to access walls for painting.

Baseboard Cleaning
When we move your heavy furniture, we'll also clean the dust and soil from exposed baseboards!

Cover Floors and Furniture
All floors and furniture will be covered with tarps to protect them from paint. Please remove knick-knacks and china from any furniture you want moved.

Draperies and Blinds
All draperies and blinds, not including rods, will be removed and replaced during painting.

Light Preparation
All minor nail holes will be filled in preparation for paint.

Pre-Treatment
Walls are pretreated with light sanding and cleaned to give a superior final finish coat.

Professional Vacuuming

A commercial, heavy-duty vacuum will be used to remove dry, abrasive, gritty, fiber damaging soils upon completion.

Walk Through and Certificate of Satisfaction
Final walk through inspection provided for complete satisfaction and final approval.

Premium Paint
Upgrade to two coats of Premium Top of the Line Paint including 1 Year Warranty Protection with Spot damage on up to 4 trips.

Colour Consultation
Professional colour consultation to help customer choose colours to best suit their decorating.

$1,950.00

BURNMAC SERVICES
"To Exceed Customer Expectations"

Gold Plus Package # 2

Furniture Moving
Furniture will be carefully moved and replaced to access walls for painting.

Baseboard Cleaning
When we move your heavy furniture, we'll also clean the dust and soil from exposed baseboards!

Cover Floors and Furniture
All floors and furniture will be covered with tarps to protect them from paint. Please remove knick-knacks and china from any furniture you want moved.

Draperies and Blinds
All draperies and blinds, not including rods, will be removed and replaced during painting.

Light Preparation
All minor nail holes will be filled in preparation for painting.

Pre-Treatment
Walls are pretreated with light sanding and cleaned to give a superior final finish coat.

Professional Vacuuming

A commercial, heavy-duty vacuum will be used to remove dry, abrasive, gritty, fiber damaging soils upon completion.

Walk Through and Certificate of Satisfaction
Final walk through inspection with customer for complete satisfaction and final approval.

Premium Paint
Upgrade to two coats of Premium Top of the Line Paint including 1 Year Warranty Protection with Spot damage on up to 4 trips.

$1750.00.00

BURNMAC SERVICES
"To Exceed Customer Expectations"

Gold Package # 3

Furniture Moving
Furniture will be carefully moved and replaced to access walls for painting.

Baseboard Cleaning
When we move your heavy furniture, we'll also clean the dust and soil from exposed baseboards!

Cover Floors and Furniture
All floors and furniture will be covered with tarps to protect them from paint. Please remove knick-knacks and china from any furniture you want moved.

Draperies and Blinds
All draperies and blinds, not including rods, will be removed and replaced during painting.

Light Preparation
All minor nail holes will be filled in preparation for paint.

Pre-Treatment
Walls are pretreated with light sanding and cleaned to give a superior final finish coat.

Two Coats of Paint
Two coats of deluxe wall paint will be provided to all walls detailed on estimate.

Professional Vacuuming
A commercial, heavy-duty vacuum will be used to remove dry, abrasive, gritty, fiber damaging soils upon completion.

Walk Through and Certificate of Satisfaction
Final walk through inspection with customer for complete satisfaction and final approval.

$1,499.00

Using these packages as illustrated will serve a few very important processes in your business. It will raise your overall profitability and separate you from your competition because of the three following reasons.

1. A certain percentage of customers will buy your **Platinum** package that will bring in more profits.
2. A certain percentage of customers will buy your **Gold Plus** package that will increase your profits.
3. You now have your customer focused on all the procedures you will provide with your service and this will have them focusing on you rather than on a competitors bid.

Make note that in the package illustration I did not name the three packages, **Best, Average,** and **Budget**. They were named **Platinum**, **Gold Plus,** and **Gold**. Presenting the packages this way gives them a higher perceived value. This selling and closing model can substantially raise your profits without creating a lot more physical work.

If you need any help with this cash driving strategy just go to www.burnmac.com.

COMMODITY MAKES ME FEEL SO CHEAP

Let me start by explaining the difference between the two ways of operating your company and selling your home service. We'll start with the example of coffee beans. If you were to buy a couple of coffee beans that are a commodity, they might cost you 2 cents. If McDonalds took those two coffee beans and brewed them, they are still a commodity, but now you are paying 95 cents for a cup of coffee. If you now took those two coffee beans and had Starbucks brew them, they would charge you $3.50 for a latte.

Why would any one pay that much extra for these lonely coffee beans? The reason is that they are paying for the experience. Keep in mind here that Starbucks is the largest coffee shop company in the world. They are growing in size and also growing in number of locations and increasing their volume of business. They just keep getting bigger and bigger.

Can you imagine Howard Schultz explaining his new coffee concept to bankers or investors when he was first getting started? He would be telling them that he wanted to open up coffee shops where the average cup of coffee would cost over twice as much as the competition. They must have thought he was crazy.

Howard Shultz understands the secret to running a profitable coffee business and does it masterfully. He knows that if you are just like every other coffee shop, you are nothing more than a commodity. He also knows that if people are buying what they think is just a commodity, than they will buy it from the cheapest shop.

Howard Shultz knows that if he provides value and an exceptional customer experience, customers will reward him, his business, and his employees handsomely. Howard does not keep this secret of value and experience guarded. In fact he has written a book telling everyone how to do it.

Remember, it is only secret information because there are very few business people using this information to their advantage, even though it is available through books like as this one and Howard Shultz's book, "Pour Your Heart into It." Even the title is an indication of the powerful energy waves that the Starbucks radio is broadcasting on. He puts

love into his business and customers and that is the highest
energy you can run a business on.

A great company like Starbucks does the following:

- Gets the best coffee beans money can buy
- Has beans roasted to excruciatingly exacting
  standards
- Hires the best architects you can buy to design each
  individual restaurant
- Has architectural design done for each neighbour-
  hood so that each restaurant better fits in
- Has high-end furniture and equipment regardless of
  money
- Offers training that is second to none for their
  baristas
- Listens to their customers because they know the
  customer is the best unpaid consulting you can ask
  for
- Has the rich smell of roasted coffee beans in the
  restaurant and goes to great lengths to make sure that
  smell is not contaminated by other odours such as
  food cooking a microwave
- Is particularly selective in the music they choose to
  play in their locations
- Is very clean

There are many more things Howard Shultz does for his customers that are available in his book, but I wanted to highlight
a few to make a dramatic point. What message, vibrational
energy, or radio station are Howard Shultz and Starbucks
broadcasting on? It is obvious when you look at the above

list that he cares about his customers. He would not go to all that extra effort and spend the higher costs if he did not love his customers. The experience and value you feel when you go to Starbucks is second to none. You trust them and know you are dealing with a very successful company.

In contrast, an "unconscious" company like Bozo's Coffee does the following:

- Buys the very cheapest coffee beans in order to save money
- Finds the cheapest way or person to roast their coffee beans
- Does not hire an architect because they know that they can probably save money by getting the landlord to do the leasehold for the new restaurant when they sign a 5-year lease
- Purchases all furniture and equipment in the cheapest way they can buy and may even consider buying at auction
- Barely offers training for their kitchen and wait help
- Does not listen to their customers because they know more than the customers do
- Has the smell of hot pastrami sandwiches wafting through the restaurant from the microwave fan, which totally kills the concept of a specialty coffee restaurant
- Hires a part time, untrained server that plays inappropriate music very loudly
- Leaves half of the tables littered from previous customers which looks very unappetizing to new people looking for clean tables

What message, vibrational energy, or radio station is Bozo's Coffee shop broadcasting on? It is obvious when you look at the above statements that they do not give a &i#% about their customers. If they loved their customers they would give them something of value. They are more interested in putting the money into their own pocket and will not spend one extra penny that they don't have to.

It is ironic that business people who run shops like Bozo's Coffee do things like this to save money but wind up with the complete opposite result. There is the saying that goes, "whatever you want, give it away." If you want your customers to love you than you had better love them first.

THE CHEAP COMMODITY LIFESTYLE STINKS!

In the mid 1990's, I read a book called "The Millionaire Next Door." I loved this book and even bought several copies to give to friends and business associates. Today I have to apologize to those people for leading them down the wrong track.

This was a book that had uncovered who millionaires were and type of a lifestyle they were living. It said that the majority of millionaires had become millionaires by being frugal and buying two or three year old used cars instead of new ones.

It said that most millionaires were not the people spending wildly on Rodeo Drive shopping sprees and driving Ferraris, but were instead small business owners who scrimped and saved their way to a million dollars. The author went on to say that even their children were not aware that their parents were millionaires because they lived in average neighbourhoods and often parked their company work trucks in the driveway.

At the time, this was a great relief to me because I had made a huge amount of money when I was younger and was finding it difficult to keep up a high-income lifestyle. This is just what I needed because now I could still be an average millionaire like the others and all I had to do was live a more frugal lifestyle.

There was only one problem with this. I know now that my problems are actually opportunities and blessings. The big problem was I hated living the "Millionaire Next Door" lifestyle. I was driving around older cars and at one point didn't even have a car and drove one of the company trucks.

Soon I had friends telling me how I could save money by buying things cheaper. I could beat people down on their suggested price and barter with the best of them. I worried about every penny and held on so tight to money that you would have thought I was penniless. I had money in the bank and a beautiful house, but I worried more and more about holding on to my money. The tighter I held on the more miserable I became.

It was without a doubt the worst time of my life. Not only did I not like living that way, but also my family had been traumatized. I laugh about it now and call it our shame therapy period. I tell my family we are now stronger because of it but I don't think they bought into my optimistic outlook about that era.

I now think that "The Millionaire Next Door" is the worst book I have ever read. Although the author was merely pointing out how most millionaires live, I took it as the way I should live because I liked being a millionaire.

The good news is that as a great marketer you don't have to live a "Millionaire Next Door" lifestyle where you may be worth a million dollars but you are still living a life of limits. As a great marketer you live a life of prosperity and realize that you don't have to barter someone out of his or her money so that you can have it all.

In your customer service experience, your intentions should focus on how you can add to the customer's experience and create more value for them. When you create a better experience for the customer they will pay a higher price and you both win.

EXPERIENCE OR COMMODITY?

One Will Make you Stupid And Broke And The Other Can Buy Your Wife A Mercedes

It is not that hard to stand out from the crowd and sell the experience. Study and practice ways that will make your customer's experience the best they have ever had. It takes dedication to make this effort each and every day until you start getting the return you desire.

Home service industry workers think that because they have a lot of competition they don't need to put their best foot forward. This is just not true and it's amazing how many think this way.

As of this writing it is time to clean up the property around my home. I want all the weeds pulled out, the deck and stairs painted, and new bark mulch added to designated areas. I phoned services for bids and only one called me back. His phone manner was terrible and he complained that it would cost gas money to come out and give me an estimate. He showed up in a rusty truck and did not have a business card.

He asked me how much I thought I should pay. I asked him to write up on an invoice with what he was including for the price he would quote. I asked him to do that twice before he started. In the end he did not do this for me and later ran into problems when he tried to remember what was included in the price. My wife asked why I had chosen to use him and I told tell her that he was the only one to even respond.

He went on to make many more customer service mistakes and I would not recommend him. Had someone better come along, and I would have been happy to pay twice the price. With very little effort on his part, this handy man could have increased his net profit easily by 500%.

Where else can you get a return like this? If you were to go to medical school, you are looking at a minimum of seven years of extra education. If you spent those seven years paying an estimated $20,000.00 per year for tuition, you still might only be earning in the $100,000.00 to $150,000.00 per year income range. Being a doctor can be very rewarding but it can also be very stressful.

Compare this situation to that of a marketer and customer service professional and you have a no brainer. If you follow all the marketing silver bullets in this book which costs approximately $25.00, get a minimum of two months of coaching from a qualified coach and purchased and studied the work book and home study business program available through my company at www.servicebusinessriches.com, chances are you would quickly exceed the income of a doctor.

The time spent learning marketing and customer service skills would equal 1/15th the time of what a doctor has to put into their education in order to start practicing. The expenses would be far below 1/20th and the increased income could be as much as three to fifteen times higher. I encourage you to take action and use this information because it is effective. You must also realize that it is not going to work until you take action, so go out and get started. Once you know how to be a marketer and customer service professional, it will pay you enormous dividends for life.

To become a commodity in the home service business is probably the most expensive way you can ever run a business. If people buy your service strictly by price then you are on the fast track to being broke and stupid. Don't pass go and head straight into bankruptcy jail. The customer that buys by the lowest price tends to have the following characteristics:

1. Price-buyers take all of your sales time
2. They do all the complaining
3. They "forget" to pay you
4. They tell your other customers how little they paid you
5. They drive off your good customers
6. They are not going to buy from you again
7. They'll require you to "invest up" to supply their needs — and then they'll blackmail you for a better price
8. They'll destroy the credibility of your price and your product
9. They will steal any ideas, designs, drawings, information, and knowledge they can get their hands on

These are not the customers you want to do business with. If you let them they will break your spirit, drive, and bank account. Don't let your customer be in the driver's seat because you are the lowest priced company. If you set yourself apart from the competition and utilize good marketing strategies, you will never find yourself in a position where you have to deal with price conscious customers.

Chapter 20

Continuity Is The Glue For Maintenance

YOU'RE ALREADY THERE, WHAT DON'T YOU UNDERSTAND?

At a recent Dan Kennedy information-marketing seminar, Dan told us that he thought that one of the most important discoveries he had made in recent years was continuity programs. In fact, Dan said that he would not even consider getting into a new business unless there was a continuity component to it.

A continuity program is a program that sets up a customer on a monthly or annual basis and is only discontinued when the customer cancels the program with the vendor. Dan has said he has left millions on the table in the past because he has not set up continuity programs for some of his businesses.

It does not take a lot to realize why continuity programs are so desirable. Most of the labour and the least amount of profit is in the first sale with a new customer. It makes sense that if you have something that you can supply to the customer automatically on a monthly basis it will mean less effort and more money for you.

Any time we hear the terms less effort and more money we should listen very carefully. You can use a continuity program for any home service business. It can take on many different forms. The one we use in our business is a maintenance program.

After we have completed work for a customer we let them know that we provide additional services like carpet and upholstery cleaning. If they are happy with our service they will usually oblige.

It is during the transaction when we ask the customer how often they like to get their carpets cleaned. Depending on the traffic situation in their home, we recommend once or twice per year with smaller service options available in between regular cleanings.

This type of maintenance program is also used in our commercial carpet cleaning division and it, too, is very effective. It is good for both the customer and our company. The customer doesn't have to worry about cleaning maintenance and we have locked in a repeat customer until they call us to cancel their service.

The effort is now on the customer to take the initiative to call up and cancel their service with us. If we are exceeding their expectations and doing certain things to make them stay with our company, the chances of them cancelling are very low.

The customer pays a small monthly fee and it is one job they never have to worry about again. This is a great value to a lot of customers because they know that it can take a lot of time and effort to find a good service company.

If you are practicing some of your persuasion techniques it is almost impossible for your customer to let you go. If your company likes them as a customer and treats them as the most important people then they will not let you go. As Mary Kay use to say, "Treat Your Customer As The Most Important People On Earth."

Make sure you are keeping in touch with your customers and send out Christmas and Birthday cards and any other number of things to stay in touch with them. A small gift to say thank you for being a great customer will pay big dividends all.

There you have two very powerful persuasion techniques. It would be very hard for a customer to pick up the phone and cancel your service. I have not even talked about consistency yet, which is the commitment the customer will make by hiring your company. We will get into this one in a bit.

I have seen how powerful these persuasion techniques can be. Even though I am consciously aware of them I sometimes have a hard time turning down companies who apply them. I was recently considering managing most of my own investments because I think I now have a good knowledge of how to do it. The person who does my investing is an expert. He "Is on TV" and writes a column for the newspaper. He is a really nice guy who always sends birthday and Christmas cards as well as books that he knows I will like. Could I pull my money out and leave him? The answer is probably no because he is just too nice a guy and is good at what he does.

EVERY SALE X 10?

Figure out a way to include a continuity program as a part of your home service system. You will automatically increase your sales by ten fold. If every customer you see is set up a continuity program, then you already have next years sales set up on auto pilot before you even get there.

While your competition is working each year to get new sales you will already have next years sales booked and be working on increasing sales and adding new continuity programs. You will dwarf your competition.

Incorporate this strategy into your sales system so that is automatic each time you make a sale. Each sale turns into a long-term customer. Customer acquisition is costly and labour intensive, but when you have a system in place to sign them up for life in the beginning you are on your way to building the biggest game in town.

I listen to a marketing teleseminar each month where a new entrepreneur is interviewed. The interviewer is a fellow who runs the marketing information newsletter I belong to. This particular month the interviewer was talking to a marketer who had made hundreds of millions of dollars selling fitness equipment. He was a well-known person and was rightfully proud of how well he had done.

The interviewer asked how big his customer list was and he said it was 4 million strong. Yes, you read it right, 4 million customers. The interviewer then asked what kind of continuity program he had for his customers? To a shocked and horrified interviewer, this fellow relayed that he did not have a continuity program.

When he was told what benefit a good continuity program could be, the interview took a turn. He realized that if even one in four of his customers signed up for a monthly continuity program it could mean millions each month that would automatically be paid to him.

For example, if he had a newsletter for $29.95 per month and sent it to 1 million people, that would turn into a 30 million dollar per month profit. There are any number of continuity programs he could implement and when he realized he could be leaving 100 million dollars a month or more on the table, he was shocked.

It would not require much effort at all for this fellow to come up with a continuity program. I am sure that as I write this that he is already well on his way.

"The Cash Is In Continuity."

—*Bob Burnham*

Think of a way to put a continuity program into your business today. If you think that it is not possible to do that, then I think I have to agree with Dan Kennedy and you should not be in that business.

MOST BUSINESSES ARE SITTING ON DIAMOND MINES

You will find that most businesses are sitting on virtual money printing presses or diamond mines. When you see a situation like the fitness equipment marketer missing out on a bigger part of the business than the one he had made hundreds of millions from, it makes you realize that most if not all of us leave a lot of money on the table each and every day.

Stand back and take a look at your business and see if there is anywhere you can automatically boost your sales. A good mentor or coach with good marketing sense can help you to see a whole new world. Memberships, newsletters, maintenance programs, and clubs are just a few of the many services you can provide to your customers on a continuity program.

You could even ask your customers what they want. Your customers will tell you and they are your best-unpaid consultants. Companies pay millions each year to consultants for this information while the best consultants are free.

Consultants don't have the insight that your customers have about working with your company.

Every time a customer complains to you it is a time to learn a life changing strategy. Most companies dismiss the whining and complaining customers as unreasonable and don't pay any attention to them.

Listen and thank them for their input. Be open and look for the little diamond mine in what they say. It is through the harsh polishing of diamonds that the sparkle starts to shine through.

Our customers are trying to tell us something but most of us are not listening. Don't forget that for every one customer who vocalizes something, there are another twelve or more who are thinking the same thing but who won't say anything. You must listen and be open to finding the gems.

You can send a questionnaire out and give them something for taking the time to fill it out. Ask them if there is a specific way you can improve your business and what that is. You could also ask them what their most pressing question is so that you could provide an answer.

You will find a pattern very quickly in your responses and come up with some great ways to serve your customers even better. Our customers do know us the best. You have to be open enough to listen to them. This approach establishes trust and lets them know they are important to you.

Always be on the hunt for ways to better service your customers and set them up on continuity programs. Your employees are a good source of ideas for continuity programs as well. Anyone on the front lines with your customers each and everyday can be a wealth of ideas and knowledge.

MORE VALUE NOT LABOUR

When you are selling a continuity program, always try to give the customer more value for the program as opposed to something that requires more labour. Value is more profitable than labour. You want to set up your continuity programs to make great profits and give your customers the best value.

I can give you a couple of examples of how you are supplying value rather than labour. In the carpet cleaning division of our company we offer a maintenance continuity program to keep their carpet clean all year. If we were to sell a continuity program and the premium, bonus, or incentive to sign up was for us to do extra cleaning, then we would be supplying more labour for them to go for the deal.

If, on the other hand, we let them have our deodorizing and sanitizing package included with the cleaning it would not require any further labour but we would still be giving them something of value that does not cost us much. We can deodorize and sanitize in the same process while we are cleaning and so no further labour is required.

Another example would be charging a monthly fee for a home service rather than including extra trips and labour. You could include something tangible that will give them more value. It could be the use of your service contacts list that they could use if they need another kind of service.

These are all examples of increased value for your customer that does not increase you cost by much.

Warranties can be of value to a customer and cost you little to maintain as opposed to how much you can sell them for. I don't think you can leave a car dealership or an electronics store without the additional warranty or maintenance program these days.

The return on investment on some of these warranties is very high for the retailer. You will notice in some of the big box retailers that you have to initial refusal of the extra warranty. This is to verify that their sales people are explaining it to all the customers because it is such a big profit center for them.

All these subtle little changes in the way you do business with your customer will bring you incredible results. When you give more value than labour you save yourself time and money.

Chapter 21

Boy, We're A Crazy Bunch

COMMITMENT REALLY IS WHAT IT USED TO BE

The last principle that Robert Cialdini talks about in his book is consistency. This principle states that with **Commitment or Consistency,** people will be more prone to move in a particular direction if they see it as being consistent with their previous commitment. Most of us keep our commitments and it can be a powerful motivator for anyone who makes a commitment.

He gives a terrific example of how the toy industry was stumped by how slow their industry is in January and February, right after the Christmas holiday. This is a real problem and required ideas on how to get customers back into the toy stores during this time. Parents are usually completely spent out and do not want to spend any more money after Christmas.

The solution that some of the toy stores and manufacturers came up with is brilliant. As you know, there is always a toy that has great appeal and that all the kids want for Christmas. This toy is heavily advertised and usually found at the top of most kids Christmas lists. The kids ask their parents if they can have this particular toy for Christmas and the parents sometimes would say yes.

The commitment is made by the unsuspecting parent to buy their children this particular present. The toy stores know that the children have their parents committed to getting them the hottest toy of the Christmas season. With this knowledge, the manufacturer purposely does not stock enough of the toys in order to handle the demand for Christmas.

The loving parents wind up buying the children an alternative present for Christmas morning, and all is fine until the ad for this particular toy shows up on TV again in mid-January. Their children remind them again that they were promised the toy that is once again being advertised on TV.

Cialdini gives another example of a restaurant that was having a lot of customers call for reservations who would later not show up. Empty tables can be a costly situation for any restaurant. The solution was quite simple.

When the customer called in to book the reservation, the hostess asked the customer to please call back if they had to cancel. If the customer said they would in fact call, they had the commitment they needed for the customer to follow his word and call back if they had to cancel. This request of the customer's commitment cut the no-show up rate by 75%.

Most people keep their commitments, and this can be a powerful way for you to do business with your customers. When you are booking work, appointments, or even picking up your payment, use the power of commitment from the customer to keep their word. Never be loose in your appointments or processes.

When you make an appointment with your customers, be specific and ask them to commit to those times, agreements, or whatever it is you are doing. Tell your customer that you will be at their home at 2 PM and then ask for their commitment to call you if they have to cancel. You will get more customers to follow through on their commitment.

It is a marketing strategy that will result in committed customers who will be more diligent in their dealings with you and they will really appreciate you for it.

You will want to practice this commitment strategy in your own business, especially when it comes to pricing your service. Before giving a quote, ask your customer if they like dealing with companies who are more service-valued as opposed to just offering the cheapest price. Most customers will tell you they like the service value company better and this sets a commitment in their mind.

It is very hard for the customer to change their opinion on their own commitment to you after the wheels have been set in motion. Get that commitment from them a few times and in a few different ways. We really do train our customers how to treat us.

Chapter 22

Accounts Receivable. I don't Think So

YOU MEAN TO TELL ME THE CUSTOMERS DON'T KNOW WHAT TO DO?

One area you can get instant results from in your home service business is in the area of accounts receivable. Many small and even medium sized businesses unknowingly commit themselves to being a bank for 30, 60, or even 90 days or more all because they are teaching their customers bad habits.

Most small businesses don't realize the cost of not getting paid right away. They don't know an easy way to avoid this from happening. If a small home service business invoices $75,000.00 worth of completed work in a month and then does not get paid for two months, this is like taking a $75,000.00 loan out to fund your customer's work for the balance of the time it takes to get paid. This is painful and completely unnecessary.

Many home service businesses suffer greatly from their past due accounts receivable list and the worst of it is they set the customer up to work with them this way. I have seen this problem turned around on a dime if you make a few quick adjustments.

In our business, we set the customer up into doing the right thing t at the time of payment. During the transaction, we have the customer do a walk through of their home after the work is complete to make sure they are 100 % happy. It is then that we ask if they would like us to put a cheque number on the invoice or if would they rather pay by Visa or MasterCard.

I have worked with many services over the years and so many of them send me an invoice or just leave an invoice after they have completed the work. This behavior will over time, qualify you for the stupid and broke village idiot award and is will be your own fault.

Every customer has a different thought as to when they think this invoice should be paid. A few will pay your invoice right away. A few more will pay in 30, 60, or 90 day's time. Some will find a problem with your work and not tell you about it until you call them up a few months later to try and collect on your invoice.

The customer does not know really when they are expected to pay and you are making so much more work and cost to yourself by doing it this way. Here are the extra costs incurred by being the village idiot:

1. Extra time calling customers to collect money
2. Extra cost of carrying money that the customer owes you
3. Possible reissuing of an invoice because payment has been left so long
4. Possible unintentional bad vibes leaving payment and having to call back
5. If left too long, they could move or not have the money

The best time to collect is at the completion of work because this is the time when they are most happy with your service. You need to let your customers know what to expect and they will be very happy to comply, especially when you have done such a great job for them.

If you are in the middle of an accounts receivable problem, you should take an aggressive action immediately to clean it up and get it back under control. Maintaining rapport with a client or customer who can't or won't pay their bills is of little value, and if left alone, collection problems tend to get much worse.

It is a matter of putting in place a system to collect payment and not allowing your customers to dictate how and when they will pay you. You can be paid in advance if you want to set it up this way. I have had some businesses say that collecting money and having no accounts receivable is impossible.

The funny thing is that while they are saying that can't be done, we are doing it each and every day with no problem. Don't ignore your accounts receivable problems. Get a handle on them right away.

In business today, even large established corporations can and do find themselves in trouble and even in bankruptcy. In situations like this, it can take years to recover only a small percentage of your money.

Companies that would have been granted credit in the past with no questions asked have gone bankrupt, leaving financial shipwrecks in their wake. Don't let this happen to your company. You hold the key to when you will get paid you just have to implement policies and systems and start your engines. Get paid now and think long and hard before accepting a customer where you may have to take on the extra task of collections.

Many significant improvements in most businesses are the result of solving problems that reared their ugly heads, often at the worst possible times.

In "Think and Grow Rich," Napoleon Hill wrote, "In every adversity lies the seed of an equal or greater opportunity."

Most business problems will have marketing-related solutions. To be very simple, increased sales will solve most problems. The success of a business is closely related to how much energy, time, and money its leaders can direct to their marketing plan as opposed to how much is consumed by internal problems.

YOU ARE NOT A BANK

You are not a bank to your customers and should not put your company in a position of holding accounts receivable when you just don't have to. You have to take your customers by the hand and let them know in a positive way when it is that you want to be paid. They will actually thank you for it and have a more positive experience if you help them with the payment process.

I don't know why home service business owners expect the customer to know when, where, and how to pay the bill. Most residential customers have no idea unless you tell them. Set up a system and educate them on how it works.

This is an even a more important issue when dealing with commercial customers. Remember that as many as 95% of all businesses go broke within their first years. You don't want to be lending companies money if there is a chance you won't get paid.

You may have a great year financially in your business and then have it ruined because a large commercial account can't pay their bill. It happens and it happens a lot. Be very clear with your commercial accounts and make sure you are going to get paid. Some may have the best of intentions but are not that good at operating their businesses and leave you holding the bag.

This even happens to large companies who suffer financial hardships when their commercial customers are unable to pay their bills. A big account can look very appealing to take on, but if they don't pay you it can be a nightmare. Don't be afraid to lose an account that cannot satisfy their payment terms.

Sometimes in business it can be the things you don't do, as well as the things you do that can make a big impact on you bottom line. Financing your customers is just not good business decision. You are not in the finance business so don't do it, especially when it is just not necessary.

Customers will always be happy to pay sooner rather than later as long as you tell them what to do. They are always willing to pay for your service when they are the happy with your work. The time to get paid is now and both you and your customer will be happier.

Chapter 23

Action Trumps Meditation

CHEERFUL EXPECTANCY

Although I meditate each and every morning and highly recommend it to all (especially home service business people), I have to make one very important point. If you don't take action, then nothing will happen. Once your thoughts are focused and the plan is laid out, you must take action to make your dreams come to fruition.

If you have a good plan and follow some or all of the strategies in this book with a positive attitude, you will come to have a life that will is full of wealth, good health, and success. This is not rocket science, but you must take action on the thoughts and strategies and implement them into your business.

I don't think there has ever been a better time in history to make as much money as you can make from a home service business. There is more help available than ever before to keep you on target.

As was discussed earlier in this book, the only thing that can stop you from achieving massive success is your own self-limiting beliefs. With the right attitude and the right actions you are assured that the success that you so desire will be on its way.

Many people who need lots of help don't receive any because of any number of reasons. In contrast, there are many people who are already very successful and who continue each and every day to learn more ways to stay that way. Even though these successful people may be at the top of their field they still go to seminars, read books, listen to CD's, and find other ways to get better at what they do.

You will encounter some naysayer's along your path that will try to bring you down to their level and you must run from them as fast as you can. You want to hang around and associate with the people who are contributing positively to society.

You will want to ask yourself this question many times per day. I call it

The Most Important Question:

"Is what I am doing right now, motion, or is it advancing me?"

This question should be kept on a piece of paper in your wallet, in your car, and on your desk. It should be read several times a day. The importance of this question should not be underestimated. If you are doing something that is motion that means that you are not advancing your business. In my business, this would include things like painting walls, fixing doors, or cleaning carpets. When you are doing things like making sales, training, marketing, or motivating, you are doing something that is increasing the value of your business and this is advancing you.

Most people do the same thing day in and day out and expect different results. Another reason to keep asking yourself this question continually is to evolve your business. We have the capacity as individuals to reach any goals we desire, as long as we stay focused on the important rather than on the urgent issues.

A PHYSICAL ASSET AND A MENTAL ASSET

It is your customer list that is the biggest asset for your business. A customer list is a prized asset and should always be growing. You can lose every other material asset in your business but your customer list can bring it all back in a very short amount of time.

Another asset that should be nurturing is the information that you have in your conscious and subconscious mind. This information can never be taken from you and more can always be added.

There are so many people that will not think twice about buying a new $40,000.00 car but won't even consider investing in a $2,500.00 seminar that could change their lives forever. A car depreciates by as much as half in the first year of ownership. Many of us spend time and money washing and maintaining our vehicles and yet won't spend any time or money on our education.

I can guarantee that if you spent $40,000.00 wisely educating yourself on how to better run your business and provide more value to your customers, you will start to see big returns. You could take that same $40,000.00 and double, triple, or even quadruple it in a very short time.

Be the one in the winning camp creating value by helping your customers live better lives and living as we were born and meant to live: **Wealthy, Healthy, and Successful. Go for it!**